Cook's Corner

Cook's
Bible

igloobooks

igloobooks

Published in 2018
by Igloo Books Ltd
Cottage Farm
Sywell
NN6 0BJ
www.igloobooks.com

Copyright © 2018 Igloo Books Ltd

All rights reserved. No part of this publication may be
reproduced or transmitted in any form or by any means,
electronic, or mechanical, including photocopying, recording,
or by any information storage and retrieval system,
without permission in writing from the publisher.
The measurements used are approximate.

Food photography and recipe development:
© Stockfood, The Food Media Agency
Cover image: © iStock / Getty Images
Additional imagery: © iStock / Getty Images

STA002 0218
2 4 6 8 10 9 7 5 3 1
ISBN: 978-1-78810-181-3

Cover designed by Nicholas Gage
Interiors designed by Simon Parker
Edited by Jasmin Peppiatt

Printed and manufactured in China

Cook's Corner

Cook's Bible

Contents

Cook's Corner

Cook's Bible
Breakfasts

Croissants

MAKES: 20 | PREP TIME: 2 HOURS | COOKING TIME: 15 MINUTES

INGREDIENTS

625 g / 1 lb 5 oz / 2 ¾ cups strong white (bread) flour

12 g salt

75 g / 3 oz / ⅓ cup sugar

20 g dried yeast

500 g / 1 lb / 2 cups butter, cold, cubed

1 egg, beaten

METHOD

1. Place the flour, salt, sugar and yeast in a bowl and add enough water to make a pliable dough. Tip onto a floured surface, and knead for 5–8 minutes. Refrigerate for 1 hour.

2. After 1 hour, remove the dough from the fridge and roll it out on a floured surface into a 60 x 30 cm (24 x 12 in) rectangle.

3. Roll out the butter into a 20 x 30 cm (8 x 12 in) rectangle and place in the middle of the dough so it covers two thirds. Fold the remaining dough third over the butter layer. Wrap in cling film and refrigerate for 1 hour.

4. Flour the work surface and roll the dough out again to 60 x 30 cm (24 x 12 in). Repeat the folding process, then refrigerate again for another hour. Repeat twice more, wrap in more cling film and rest overnight. Roll out the dough to around 3 mm thickness and cut into 20 x 20 cm (8 x 8 in) squares.

5. Cut each square into two triangles and place on a lightly floured surface. Roll each dough triangle up and curl round to make the traditional crescent shape. Place on lined baking trays and leave to rise for 1 hour in warm place. Preheat the oven to 200°C (180°C fan) / 400F / gas 6.

6. Lightly brush with beaten egg and bake for about 15 minutes or until crisp.

Eggs benedict

SERVES: 4 | PREP TIME: 10 MINUTES | COOKING TIME: 3-5 MINUTES

INGREDIENTS

4 eggs

4 thick slices ham

4 English muffins

30 g butter

FOR THE HOLLANDAISE SAUCE:

175 g / 6 oz / ¾ cup butter

1 tbsp white wine vinegar

2 tbsp lemon juice

3 egg yolks

pinch of salt

METHOD

1. Melt the butter in a pan. Place the vinegar and lemon juice in another pan and boil.

2. Place the egg yolks and salt in a food processor and whizz briefly, then with it still running, very gradually add the hot lemon juice and vinegar.

3. Again very slowly add the melted butter until the sauce emulsifies. Keep warm in a bowl over hot water while you cook the eggs.

4. Poach the eggs in boiling water for about 3 minutes for a runny yolk. Remove to kitchen paper and leave to drain.

5. Cut the muffins in half horizontally and lightly toast the cut sides, then butter.

6. Place the muffins on a plate and lay over the slices of ham.

7. Top with the poached eggs and hollandaise sauce.

Breakfast frittata

SERVES: 6 | PREP TIME: 15 MINUTES | COOKING TIME: 35 MINUTES

INGREDIENTS

8 eggs

1 tbsp crème fraîche

2 tbsp olive oil

4 good quality pork sausages, meat removed from the skins and cut into small chunks

4 rashers smoked streaky bacon, chopped

100 g / 3 ½ oz / ½ cup button mushrooms, thickly sliced

12 cherry tomatoes, quartered

½ bunch parsley, chopped

salt and pepper

METHOD

1. Preheat the oven to 180°C (160°C fan) / 350F / gas 5.

2. Beat the eggs with the crème fraîche in a large bowl.

3. Heat the oil in a pan and cook the sausage chunks and bacon until golden.

4. Add the mushrooms and cook briskly until all the liquid evaporates, then add the tomatoes.

5. Pour the egg mixture in and distribute evenly.

6. Bake for about 35 minutes until puffed and golden. The egg should be fully cooked through.

7. Cut into squares and serve warm or cold.

Apple, honey and walnut porridge

SERVES: 4 | PREP TIME: 10 MINUTES | COOKING TIME: 25 MINUTES

INGREDIENTS

2 eating apples, peeled, cored and halved

1 ½ tbsp butter

50 g / 1 ¾ oz / ½ cup walnuts, chopped

75 ml / 2 ½ fl. oz / ¼ cup manuka honey

600 ml / 1 pint / 2 ½ cups whole milk

125 g / 4 ½ oz / 1 ¼ cups rolled porridge oats

mint leaves to garnish

METHOD

1. Preheat the oven to 180°C (160°C fan) / 350F / gas 4.

2. Arrange the apples, cut side up on a large square of foil. Put 1 tsp of butter into the cavity of each one, then fold the sides of the foil up and crimp together to make a parcel.

3. Bake the apple parcel in a roasting tin for 20 minutes. Carefully undo the foil then scatter over the walnuts and drizzle with honey. Re-crimp the foil and return to the oven for 5 minutes.

4. Meanwhile, mix the milk with the oats in a saucepan, then stir over a medium heat until it starts to simmer. Add a pinch of salt then reduce the heat to its lowest setting and continue to stir for 5 minutes.

5. Divide the porridge between four bowls. Carefully unfold the apple parcels and lay a baked apple half on top of each bowl. Spoon the warm honey and walnuts over the top and serve immediately, garnished with mint.

Scrambled egg stuffed tomatoes

SERVES: 4 | PREP TIME: 10 MINUTES | COOKING TIME: 10-15 MINUTES

INGREDIENTS

6 eggs, lightly beaten

40 g butter

6 tsp double (heavy) cream

salt and pepper

1 tbsp parsley, chopped

4 large tomatoes

METHOD

1. Preheat the oven to 200°C (180°C fan) / 400F / gas 7.

2. Heat most of the butter in a pan until foaming, then stir in the eggs.

3. Cook gently, stirring thoroughly with a wooden spoon moving the eggs around the pan until lightly cooked with some liquid egg still left.

4. Stir in the cream and parsley and season.

5. Core the tomatoes and scoop a little of the flesh from inside, then spoon the egg into the cavity.

6. Place in a roasted tin and cook for 10–15 minutes or until the tomatoes have softened.

Polenta porridge

SERVES: 1 | PREP TIME: 5 MINUTES | COOKING TIME: 10 MINUTES

INGREDIENTS

100 ml / 3 ½ fl. oz / ½ cup water

75 ml / 2 ½ fl. oz / ⅓ cup milk

75 g / 2 ½ oz / ½ cup polenta

50 ml / 1 ¾ fl. oz / ¼ cup double (heavy) cream

1 tbsp honey

METHOD

1. Heat the water and milk in a saucepan over a medium heat.

2. Once warm at the polenta stirring continuously until smooth and creamy.

3. Mix through the cream and the honey to sweeten.

4. Serve immediately in a bowl. Garnish with any additional fruits and berries as you would with oat porridge.

French toast

SERVES: 4 | PREP TIME: 15 MINUTES | COOKING TIME: 10 MINUTES

INGREDIENTS

1 thick slice white bread per person

2 eggs, beaten

300 ml / 10 fl. oz / 1 ¼ cups full fat milk
or single cream

1 tsp vanilla extract

½ tsp ground cinnamon

2 tbsp vegetable oil

METHOD

1. Whisk together the eggs, milk, vanilla and
   cinnamon and pour into a bowl.

2. Lay the bread into the mixture, soaking it
   thoroughly for a few minutes.

3. Heat the oil in a pan and gently fry the bread
   triangles two at a time until golden
   and crisp on each side.

4. Serve hot.

Scrambled eggs on toast

SERVES: 4 | PREP TIME: 5 MINUTES | COOKING TIME: 8 MINUTES

INGREDIENTS

6 eggs

40 g butter

6 tsp double (heavy) cream

salt and pepper

1 tbsp chives, chopped

4 thick slices bread, toasted and buttered

METHOD

1. Crack the eggs into a bowl and beat lightly.

2. Heat most of the butter in a pan until foaming, then stir in the eggs.

3. Cook gently, stirring thoroughly with a wooden spoon moving the eggs around the pan until lightly cooked with some liquid egg still left.

4. Stir in the cream and chives and season.

5. Serve immediately with the toast.

Chocolate Belgian waffles

SERVES: 2 | PREP TIME: 10 MINUTES | COOKING TIME: 15 MINUTES

INGREDIENTS

50 g / 1 ¾ oz / ¼ cup unsalted butter

1 large egg

150 ml / 5 ¼ fl. oz / ⅔ cup milk

175 g / 6 oz / 1 ¼ cups plain (all-purpose) flour

1 tsp baking powder

50 g / 1 ¾ oz / ¼ cup caster (superfine) sugar

100 g / 3 ½ oz / ⅔ cup fresh raspberries

50 g / 1 ¾ oz / ¼ cup chocolate sauce

icing (confectioner's) sugar, to dust

METHOD

1. Turn on your waffle iron. In a small pan melt the butter and set aside to cool.

2. Whisk together the eggs and milk. Add the flour, baking powder, sugar and most of the melted butter, continuing to whisk until a light batter forms.

3. Brush the waffle iron with the remaining butter and cook the waffles in batches, placing into a low oven to keep warm.

4. To serve, place the waffles onto warmed plates and top with the berries and chocolate sauce before dusting with icing sugar.

American pancakes with blueberries

SERVES: 2 | PREP TIME: 10 MINUTES | COOKING TIME: 10 MINUTES

INGREDIENTS

150 g / 5 ¼ oz / 1 cup plain (all purpose) flour

1 tbsp sugar

1 tsp baking powder

1 egg, beaten

200 ml / 7 fl. oz / ¾ cup milk

1 tsp oil for frying

50 g / 1 ¾ oz / ⅓ cup blueberries

2 tbsp apricot jam (jelly)

METHOD

1. Preheat the oven to its lowest setting.

2. In a large mixing bowl combine the flour, sugar and baking powder.

3. Mix the egg and milk and pour into the dry ingredients. Whisk for a couple of minutes until a thick and smooth batter forms. Leave to stand for a couple of minutes.

4. Heat the oil in a non-stick frying pan over a medium high heat. Once hot, add a ladle of batter to the pan and cook for 2-3 minutes until small holes appear on the surface. Flip over and cook for a further minute before transferring to the oven to keep warm while you cook the remaining batter.

5. Serve the pancakes with the blueberries and apricot jam.

Cook's Corner

Cook's Bible

Lighter bites and lunches

Vegetable couscous

SERVES: 4 | PREP TIME: 15 MINUTES | COOKING TIME: 12 MINUTES

INGREDIENTS

250 g / 9 oz / 1 cup couscous

2 tbsp sultanas

250 ml / 9 fl. oz / 1 cup stock

squeeze of lemon juice

2 tbsp olive oil

1 clove garlic, crushed

2 carrots, peeled and thickly sliced

1 red pepper, finely chopped

1 yellow pepper, finely chopped

handful green beans

150 ml / 5 fl. oz / ⅔ cup vegetable stock

4 tomatoes, chopped

salt and pepper

½ bunch parsley, roughly chopped

2 tbsp pine nuts, toasted

METHOD

1. Place the couscous in a bowl, cover with the hot stock and cling film the bowl. Leave for 10 minutes or so until tender, then fork through the grains and add the lemon.

2. Meanwhile heat the oil in a pan and sauté the garlic, carrots and diced peppers and toss to coat and cook for 3 minutes.

3. Add the beans and cover with vegetable stock and leave to simmer for 5–8 minutes until all is tender.

4. Add the tomatoes and heat through.

5. Tip the sautéed vegetables into the couscous.

6. Season generously then add the parsley and pine nuts and serve.

Gazpacho

SERVES: 6 | PREP TIME: 1 HOUR, 20 MINUTES

INGREDIENTS

800 g / 1 ¾ lb / 3 ⅓ cups ripe tomatoes

10 cm (4 in) piece of cucumber, diced

½ bunch spring onions (scallions), finely chopped

2 cloves garlic, crushed

½ red pepper, finely chopped

1 bunch basil

100 ml / 3 ½ fl. oz / ½ cup extra virgin olive oil

1–2 tbsp red wine vinegar

300 ml ice-cold water

salt and pepper

FOR THE GARNISH:

2 spring onions (scallions), finely chopped

10 cm (4 in) piece cucumber,
finely chopped croutons

METHOD

1. Cut a cross in the skin at the bottom of the tomatoes, place in a bowl of boiling water and leave for 30 seconds. This should help the skins slip off easily.

2. Halve the tomatoes, deseed and chop the flesh and place in a food processor.

3. Add the rest of the ingredients, then whizz until smooth.

4. Pour into a bowl and adjust the seasoning if necessary.

5. Chill thoroughly for at least 1 hour before serving.

6. Check the seasoning and serve with the garnishes.

Thai chicken noodle soup

SERVES: 2 | PREP TIME: 15 MINUTES | COOKING TIME: 30 MINUTES

INGREDIENTS

4 chicken thighs, boneless and skinless

750 ml / 25 ⅓ fl. oz / 3 cups chicken stock

3 cm (1 in) root ginger, peeled and sliced

2 cloves of garlic, finely chopped

1 lemongrass stalk, bruised

1 tsp fish sauce

2 birds eye chillies (chilies), chopped

a bunch of coriander (cilantro), chopped

2 limes

1 red pepper, deseeded and sliced

2 carrots, finely sliced

75 g / 2 ½ oz rice or wheat noodles

1 tbsp soy sauce

1 tbsp sesame oil

METHOD

1. Chop the chicken into bite sized pieces and add to a large saucepan with the stock, ginger, garlic, lemongrass, fish sauce, chillies, chopped coriander stalks and juice of one lime.

2. Place onto a high heat until boiling before covering and cooking until the chicken is tender and cooked, around 20 minutes.

3. Add the peppers, carrots and noodles to the soup and cook for a further 10 minutes until the vegetables are soft and noodles cooked.

4. Stir the soy sauce and sesame oil through the soup followed by the chopped coriander leaves.

5. Serve with the remaining lime chopped into quarters.

Spinach soup

SERVES: 4-6 | PREP TIME: 15 MINUTES | COOKING TIME: 25 MINUTES

INGREDIENTS

25 g / 1 oz butter

1 leek, sliced

2 celery sticks, sliced

1 large potato, peeled and cubed

1 clove of garlic, minced

1 ltr chicken stock

25 g / 1 oz / ¼ cup pine nuts

500 g / 1 lb 1 oz spinach, washed

Salt and freshly ground black pepper

200 ml / 7 fl. oz / ¾ cup crème fraîche

METHOD

1. Heat the butter in a large saucepan until foaming. Add the leeks, celery and potato and sweat for 8-10 minutes until softened.

2. Add the garlic to the pan and cook for a further minute until fragrant before pouring the stock into the pan. Cover and cook for 10-12 minutes or until the potato is softened.

3. Add the pine nuts and spinach to the pan and continue to cook for 3-5 minutes until the spinach has wilted.

4. Blend the soup either in a stand blender or by using a hand blender until smooth. Season with salt and black pepper to taste.

5. Serve in bowls with a spoonful of crème fraîche swirled through the soup.

Herby fish cakes

SERVES: 3-4 | PREP TIME: 40 MINUTES | COOKING TIME: 10 MINUTES

INGREDIENTS

225 g / 8 oz / 1 cup white fish, salmon or tuna, cut into small cubes

225 g / 8 oz / 1 cup mashed potato

2 tbsp parsley, chopped

1 tbsp chervil, chopped

3 tsp capers, chopped (optional)

squeeze of lemon juice

salt and pepper

1 egg, beaten

3 tbsp breadcrumbs

vegetable oil

METHOD

1. Combine the fish, potatoes, herbs, capers and a little lemon juice in a bowl and season well.

2. Chill for 30 minutes.

3. Form into equal-sized patties, then dip into the egg, then the breadcrumbs.

4. Heat 1 cm (½ in) depth of oil in a pan and gently fry the fishcakes on both sides until golden and crisp.

5. Drain on kitchen paper and serve with peas and ketchup.

Rice noodle broth

SERVES: 2 | PREP TIME: 15 MINUTES | COOKING TIME: 20 MINUTES

INGREDIENTS

500 ml / 17 fl. oz / 2 cups chicken or vegetable stock

1 lemongrass stalk, thinly sliced

2 kaffir lime leaves

25 g / 1 oz root ginger, peeled and sliced

1 tsp fish sauce

2 red chillies (chilies), sliced

50 g / 1 ¾ oz / ⅓ cup garden peas

200 g / 7 oz rice noodles

1 tbsp sesame oil

1 red pepper, deseeded and sliced

1 tbsp sesame seeds

2 spring onions (scallions), sliced

METHOD

1. Place the stock into a large saucepan and add the lemongrass, lime leaves, ginger, fish sauce and chillies. Heat until boiling before turning down to a simmer and leaving to cook for 20 minutes. Add the peas for the last 5 minutes.

2. Cook the rice noodles as per the packet instructions. Drain thoroughly and drizzle over the sesame oil.

3. Place the noodles into serving bowls and ladle over the broth.

4. Place the peppers, sesame seeds and spring onions on top of the noodles and serve.

35

Flaked salmon on potato farls

SERVES: 2 | PREP TIME: 10 MINUTES | COOKING TIME: 20 MINUTES

INGREDIENTS

250 g / 9 oz mashed potato

25 g / 1 oz butter, melted

50 g / 1 ¾ oz / ⅓ cup plain (all purpose) flour

2 tbsp oil

2 x 260 g / 9 oz salmon fillets

1 tbsp olive oil

1 lemon, quartered

75 g / 2 ½ oz mixed salad leaves

METHOD

1. Mix the potato with the melted butter and flour into a smooth dough. Turn out onto a floured surface and knead briefly to bring it together. Roll out to 3mm in thickness in a rectangle shape and divide into four.

2. Heat half the oil in a large non-stick frying pan over a medium high heat. Add the potato farls and fry for 3-4 minutes on each side until golden. Place into the oven to keep warm while you cook the salmon.

3. Wash and pat the salmon fillets dry with kitchen paper and season the skin with plenty of salt.

4. Heat the oil in a non-stick frying pan over a medium high heat. Place the fish skin side down in the pan and fry for 3-5 minutes. Season the flesh side.

5. Turn the fish over and fry the other side for 2-3 minutes before squeezing over some lemon juice. Remove from the pan and pull apart the salmon using a fork, season with salt and black pepper.

6. Serve the potato farls topped with the salad and salmon.

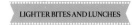

Grilled chicken with cheese

SERVES: 4 | PREP TIME: 10 MINUTES | COOKING TIME: 25 MINUTES

INGREDIENTS

4 chicken breasts

100 g / 3 ½ oz. tomato passata

1 tsp oregano

1 tsp basil

100 g / 3 ½ oz / 1 cup Cheddar cheese, grated

100 g / 3 ½ oz / 1 cup mozzarella cheese, grated

Salt and freshly ground black pepper

METHOD

1. Preheat your grill to a medium setting.

2. Trim the chicken breasts and, if large, slice in half, length ways. Season with salt and black pepper and place onto a baking tray.

3. Place the chicken under the grill and cook for 8-10 minutes on each side until browned and cooked through.

4. Mix the passata with the dried herbs and spread over one side of the chicken breasts before topping with the grated cheese.

5. Place back under the grill and cook for a further 5 minutes until the cheese has melted and started to brown.

Mushroom and mandarin salad

SERVES: 1 | PREP TIME: 10 MINUTES

INGREDIENTS

75 g / 2 ½ oz chestnut mushrooms

25 ml / ¾ fl. oz olive oil

Sea salt and cracked black pepper

1 mandarin

75 g / 2 ½ oz mixed salad leaves

METHOD

1. Thoroughly wash the mushrooms and dry with kitchen paper. Peel the skin from the top of the mushrooms before slicing.

2. Place into a bowl with 1 tbsp olive oil and the salt and pepper.

3. Zest the mandarin before peeling and separating the segments. Mix the zest and mandarin segments into the mushrooms.

4. Place the salad leaves into a bowl and top with the mushroom and mandarin mixture. Pour over the remaining oil and season with salt and black pepper.

Satay chicken

SERVES: 4 | PREP TIME: 4 HOURS | COOKING TIME: 10 MINUTES

INGREDIENTS

8 chicken thighs, boned and skinned
and cut in half

2 shallots, peeled and finely chopped

½ red chilli, finely chopped

2 cloves garlic, finely chopped

1 cm (½ in) piece fresh ginger, grated

5 tbsp peanut butter

1 tbsp tamarind paste

2 tbsp soy sauce

100 ml / 3 ½ fl. oz / ½ cup coconut milk

1 tsp palm or dark brown sugar

1 tbsp fish sauce

1 lime, juiced

METHOD

1. Mix together the marinade ingredients and
    pour half over the chicken pieces.

2. Leave to marinate for at least 4 hours
    or overnight.

3. Skewer with soaked wooden kebab sticks.

4. Griddle over a high heat until blackened in
    patches and cooked through.

5. Meanwhile heat the remaining sauce in a
    small pan, then squeeze in a little lime juice.

6. Serve the satay sauce alongside the chicken.

Chicken nuggets

SERVES: 4 | PREP TIME: 2 MINUTES | COOKING TIME: 10 MINUTES

INGREDIENTS

4 chicken breasts, skinned

300 ml / 10 fl. oz / 1 ¼ cups buttermilk

100 g / 3 ½ oz / ½ cup plain
(all-purpose) flour

2 eggs, beaten

200 g / 7 oz / ¾ cup breadcrumbs

1 tsp mustard powder

pinch of cayenne

1 tsp dried oregano

salt and pepper

vegetable oil

METHOD

1. Bash the chicken breasts between 2 pieces of cling film with a rolling pin until about 2 cm (1 in) thick.

2. Cut each piece into thick strips and place in a bowl with the buttermilk. Refrigerate for at least 2 hours or even overnight.

3. The next day, dip them one at a time into the flour, egg then breadcrumbs mixed with the flavourings and lay on a rack to dry slightly.

4. Heat 1 cm (½ in) depth oil in a pan and fry the chicken in batches until golden on both sides and cooked through.

5. Serve with a squeeze of lemon and ketchup.

Vegetable soup

SERVES: 4-6 | PREP TIME: 15 MINUTES | COOKING TIME: 20-25 MINUTES

INGREDIENTS

3 tbsp olive oil

1 large onion, chopped

2 carrots, roughly chopped

2 sticks celery, chopped 1 clove garlic, finely chopped

2 large potatoes, peeled and chopped

2 bay leaves

2 x 400 g can chopped tomatoes

1.5 litres / 3 pints / 6 ⅓ cups vegetable stock

large handful green beans, chopped

50 g / 1 ¾ oz / ¼ cup peas

salt and pepper

extra virgin olive oil

parmesan, to serve

METHOD

1. Heat the oil in a large pan and sweat the onion, carrot and celery until beginning to soften.

2. Add the potatoes, garlic and bay leaves, cook for 3 minutes, then add the tomatoes and stock and bring to a simmer.

3. Cook for 10 minutes then add the beans and peas and leave to simmer for another 6-7 minutes until they are tender.

4. Season well.

5. This soup is best served a little warmer than room temperature with extra virgin olive oil drizzled over and a generous grating of Parmesan.

43

Minestrone

SERVES: 4 | PREP TIME: 20 MINUTES | COOKING TIME: 1 HOUR 30 MINUTES

INGREDIENTS

2 tbsp olive oil

50 g / 1 ½ oz / ⅓ cup pancetta or smoked streaky bacon

1 onion, peeled and finely chopped

2 celery stalks, finely chopped

2 carrots, peeled and finely chopped

100 g / 3 ½ oz / ½ cup cauliflower, finely chopped

2 cloves garlic, finely chopped

2 potatoes, peeled and finely chopped

1.5 litres / 2 ½ pints / 5 cups chicken stock

200 g / 6 ½ oz / ¾ cup greens, such as Savoy cabbage, finely sliced

100 g / 3 ½ oz / ½ cup macaroni pasta

salt and pepper

Parmesan cheese

extra virgin olive oil

METHOD

1. Heat the oil in a large pan and fry the pancetta until the fat runs and it starts to turn golden.

2. Add the vegetables in the order given, giving each one a good 5 minutes to cook without browning, stirring regularly, before adding the next one.

3. Pour in the stock and bring to a gently simmer, then cook very gently for about an hour.

4. Add the greens and the pasta and cook for a further 30 minutes.

5. Adjust the seasoning.

6. Serve hot, warm or even room temperature sprinkled with Parmesan and drizzled with olive oil.

Shakshuka

SERVES: 2-4 | PREP TIME: 10 MINUTES | COOKING TIME: 25 MINUTES

INGREDIENTS

2 tbsp rapeseed oil

1 large onion, diced

1 red pepper, diced

2 red chillies (chilies), sliced

2 cloves of garlic, chopped

1 tsp cumin

1 tsp cayenne

1 tsp smoked paprika

1 tbsp tomato purée

400 g / 14 oz. canned chopped tomatoes

Salt and freshly ground black pepper

5 free range eggs

A small bunch of flat leaf parsley

METHOD

1. Heat the oil in a large cast iron pan with a lid over a medium heat. Add the onions and pepper and fry for 4-6 minutes until softened. Add the fresh chilli and garlic to the pan and cook for a further minute until fragrant.

2. Add the cumin, cayenne, paprika and tomato purée to the pan. Stir through the vegetables for a minute or so until fully coated. Pour the chopped tomatoes into the pan along with a splash of water and season. Cook for ten minutes until the sauce has thickened but not dried out, if it is looking a little dry mix though some more water.

3. Make 5 small dents in the surface of the sauce and break the eggs into them. Place the lid onto the pan and let the eggs poach in the sauce until the whites are cooked and the yolks still runny, this should take a couple of minutes.

4. Season with salt and black pepper and sprinkle over the chopped parsley. Serve in the pan with some tortillas or natural yogurt as desired.

Cream of tomato soup with basil

SERVES: 4 | PREP TIME: 5 MINUTES | COOKING TIME: 35 MINUTES

INGREDIENTS

500 g / 1 lb / 2 cups ripe tomatoes, halved

olive oil

salt and pepper

rosemary sprigs

4 cloves garlic

1 litre / 2 ¼ pints / 4 ¼ cups
vegetable stock

100 ml / 3 ½ fl. oz / ½ cup double
(heavy) cream

1 bunch basil leaves plus stalks

METHOD

1. Preheat the oven to 200°C (180°C fan) /
   400F / gas 7.

2. Tip the tomatoes into a roasting tin and
   drizzle with oil. Season and tuck the
   rosemary and garlic cloves in and around.

3. Roast in the oven until blackened
   and tender – about 25 minutes.

4. Remove the rosemary sprigs and discard.
   Squeeze the garlic flesh from the skins into a
   blender and carefully tip in the tomatoes and
   their juices – you may need to do this in two
   batches – and the basil stalks.

5. Add the stock and blend until smooth.

6. Return the soup to a pan and heat through
   with the cream. Heat without boiling, then
   serve decorated with torn basil leaves.

Minted pea soup

SERVES: 4 | PREP TIME: 5 MINUTES | COOKING TIME: 10 MINUTES

INGREDIENTS

25 g butter

1 onion, peeled and finely chopped

1 garlic clove, finely chopped

250 g / 9 oz / 1 cup peas, fresh or frozen

1 large potato, peeled and chopped

500 ml / 1 pint / 2 cups chicken or vegetable stock

¼ bunch mint leaves, chopped

150 ml / 5 fl. oz / ⅔ cup single cream

salt and pepper

METHOD

1. Heat the butter in a pan and sweat the onion and garlic for about five minutes without browning.

2. Add the peas, potato, stock and half the mint and bring to the boil.

3. Simmer for 5–6 minutes until the peas are tender.

4. Remove and discard the herb stalks and liquidize the soup in a blender until completely smooth.

5. Return to the heat, season and pour in the single cream. Do not allow to boil.

6. Serve in bowls, garnishing with a little chopped mint.

Prawn cocktail

SERVES: 4 | PREP TIME: 15 MINUTES | COOKING TIME: 10-14 MINUTES

INGREDIENTS

1 little gem lettuce, leaves separated

½ cucumber, finely diced

250 g / 9 oz / 1 cup North Atlantic
prawns (shrimp), cooked

FOR THE MARIE ROSE SAUCE:

4 tbsp mayonnaise

2 tbsp tomato ketchup

HOT SAUCE:

squeeze of lemon juice

salt and pepper

dash of dry sherry (optional)

½ tsp paprika, to serve

METHOD

1. Layer the lettuce, cucumber and prawns in
   individual serving glasses.

2. Mix together the ingredients for
   both the sauces, tasting as you go.
   It should not be too sickly.

3. Spoon the sauce over the prawn salad, then
   sprinkle over a little paprika before serving.

51

Asparagus risotto

SERVES: 4 | PREP TIME: 10 MINUTES | COOKING TIME: 25 MINUTES

INGREDIENTS

2 tbsp olive oil

40 g butter

1 onion, peeled and finely chopped

1 bunch asparagus, woody ends snapped off

320 g / 11 oz / 1 ⅓ cups risotto rice

100 ml / 3 ½ fl. oz / ½ cup dry white wine

1 litre / 2 ¼ pints / 4 ¼ cups chicken or vegetable stock

salt and pepper

3 tbsp butter

120 g / 4 oz / ½ cup Parmesan, grated

1 lemon, juiced and grated zest

METHOD

1. Heat the oil and butter in a large pan and add the onion and garlic. Cook until soft and translucent.

2. Chop the asparagus into short lengths and add to the pan. Cook for a few minutes.

3. Add the rice and stir to coat in the butter. Pour in the wine and stir the rice while the wine is absorbed.

4. Once the wine has cooked in, reduce the heat a little and add the hot stock, a ladleful at a time, stirring fairly continuously. This will give the risotto its creamy texture.

5. Keep stirring in the stock and tasting the rice. After about 15–20 minutes, the rice should be soft but with a slight bite. If you've run out of stock before the rice is cooked, simply use water.

6. Season and remove from the heat. Add the butter and Parmesan and leave to melt into the risotto. Stir in the lemon zest and juice.

Stuffed peppers

SERVES: 4 | PREP TIME: 30 MINUTES | COOKING TIME: 30 MINUTES

INGREDIENTS

4 green peppers, tops and seeds removed

1 onion, peeled and finely chopped

2 cloves garlic, finely chopped

1 tbsp olive oil

300 g / 10 oz / 1 ¼ cups minced beef

2 tsp chilli (chili) powder

2 tbsp tomato purée

50 g / 2 oz cooked sweetcorn

50 g / 2 oz cooked black beans

200 g / 7 oz / ¾ cup white rice, cooked

2 tbsp Cheddar cheese, grated

handful of coriander (cilantro), chopped, to serve

METHOD

1. Fry the onion and garlic in the oil until translucent.

2. Add the beef and chilli powder, turn up the heat and fry briskly, stirring, until the beef is cooked. Season.

3. Stir in the tomato purée, sweetcorn and beans, and a cup of water. Leave to simmer until the water is absorbed, then stir in the rice and leave to cool a little.

4. Preheat the oven to 200°C (180°C fan) / 400F / gas 6.

5. Fill the peppers with the beef mixture and place in a roasting tin.

6. Scatter over the cheese and bake in the oven for about 30 minutes or until they are soft but retaining their shape. Garnish with coriander before serving.

Pearl barley stuffed peppers

SERVES: 2 | PREP TIME: 15 MINUTES | COOKING TIME: 30 MINUTES

INGREDIENTS

2 red peppers, halved seeds removed

2 tbsp olive oil

1 onion, diced

2 carrots, diced

1 clove of garlic, chopped

1 aubergine (eggplant), diced

400 g / 14 oz canned chopped tomatoes

100 g / 3 ½ oz / 2/4 cup pearl barley, washed

A handful of basil leave, chopped

25 g / 1 oz / ¼ cup parmesan cheese, grated

METHOD

1. Preheat the oven to 180°C (160°C fan) / 350F / gas 4.

2. Rub half the olive oil over the peppers and season. Place onto a baking tray cut side down and bake for 20 minutes until tender.

3. Heat the remaining oil in a casserole pan and fry the onion and carrots for 5 minutes. Add the garlic and aubergine and fry for a further minute before adding the tomatoes. Simmer for 20 minutes, seasoning to taste.

4. At the same time add the pearl barley to a pan of salted boiling water and cook for 20 minutes until softened. Drain and set aside.

5. Mix three quarters of the pearl barley into the tomato and vegetable mixture and spoon into the peppers. Top with the remaining barley and bake in the oven for a further 10 minutes. Top with the herbs and cheese.

Baked chicken drumsticks

SERVES: 2-4 | PREP TIME: 10 MINUTES | COOKING TIME: 20 MINUTES

INGREDIENTS

1 kg / 2 lbs 2 oz chicken drumsticks

2 tbsp olive oil

1 tbsp dried oregano

1 tbsp dried tarragon

1 tsp chilli (chili) flakes

Salt and freshly ground black pepper

1 bulb of garlic

2 lemons, quartered

METHOD

1. Preheat the oven to 220°C (200°C fan) / 425F / gas 7.

2. Combine the chicken with the oil, herbs and chilli in a large mixing bowl, adding seasoning. Toss the ingredients together to coat the chicken in the oil and seasoning.

3. Place into an ovenproof dish. Crush the garlic with your hand and scatter the cloves around the chicken. Squeeze over some lemon and scatter the remaining wedges.

4. Bake in the hot oven for 18-20 minutes until the skin is golden and the juices run clear when the meat is pricked with a knife.

Smoked salmon mousse

SERVES: 4 | PREP TIME: 15 MINUTES | COOKING TIME: 10-14 MINUTES

INGREDIENTS

250 g / 9 oz / 1 cup smoked
salmon trimmings

100 g / 3 ½ oz / ½ cup cream cheese

2 tbsp crème fraîche

½ lemon, juiced

2 tbsp chives, chopped

salt and pepper

8–12 slices smoked salmon

lemon wedges to serve

METHOD

1. Place the ingredients in a food processor and pulse until roughly chopped.

2. Season carefully.

3. Lay 2 slices of smoked salmon out on a surface, overlapping, and place a large spoonful in the centre. Wrap the salmon around the mousse to make an enclosed parcel.

4. Place on a platter, seam side down, and repeat for the remaining salmon slices.

5. Chill until needed then serve with lemon.

Cream of courgette soup

SERVES: 1 | PREP TIME: 10 MINUTES | COOKING TIME: 20 MINUTES

INGREDIENTS

1 courgette (zucchini)

1 tbsp olive oil

1 tbsp butter

1 leek, finely chopped

1 clove of garlic, minced

150 ml / 5 ¼ fl. oz / ⅔ cup vegetable stock

50 ml / 1 ¾ fl. oz / ¼ cup double (heavy) cream

Salt and black pepper

Oil and a red chilli (chili) to garnish (optional)

METHOD

1. Peel the courgette and slice. Finely chop some of the peeled skin and reserve.

2. Heat the oil and butter, adding the leek and cook for 5 minutes until softened.

3. Add the garlic and courgette and fry for a further minute. Pour in the vegetable stock, cover and leave to cook for 10-12 minutes.

4. Pour the cream in and blend until smooth using a hand blender. Add the sliced courgette peel and season. Cook for a further 2-3 minutes and taste to check seasoning.

5. Pour into serving bowls and garnish with a drizzle of oil and a halved chilli.

Chicken schnitzel

SERVES: 4 | PREP TIME: 15 MINUTES | COOKING TIME: 10-14 MINUTES

INGREDIENTS

100 g / 3 ½ oz. / ⅔ cup panko breadcrumbs

25 g / 1 oz / ¼ cup parmesan cheese, finely grated

1 lemon, zest only

Sea salt and freshly ground black pepper

100 ml / 3 ½ fl. oz / ½ cup rapeseed oil

2 tbsp plain (all purpose) flour

2 eggs, beaten

METHOD

1. Place the chicken breasts on to a layer of cling film. Place more cling film on top and flatten the chicken using a rolling pin and cut into smaller pieces.

2. Mix panko breadcrumbs with the parmesan, lemon zest, salt and pepper.

3. Heat the oil in a large frying pan over a medium high heat.

4. Dip the chicken in the flour and then the egg before coating in the breadcrumbs. Carefully place into the hot oil and cook for 3-4 minutes on each side. Remove from the oil and place onto kitchen paper to drain.

Curried chicken chowder

SERVES: 2-4 | PREP TIME: 15 MINUTES | COOKING TIME: 40 MINUTES

INGREDIENTS

1 tbsp vegetable oil

1 tbsp olive oil

1 onion, diced

2 carrots, diced

1 clove of garlic, minced

1 tsp curry powder

1 tsp fenugreek powder

200 g / 7 oz potatoes, peeled and diced

250 ml / 8 ½ fl. oz / 1 cup chicken stock

250 ml / 8 ½ fl. oz / 1 cup milk

200 g / 7 oz cooked chicken

Sea salt and black pepper

A small bunch of fresh coriander (cilantro),
half chopped.

METHOD

1. Heat the oil and butter in a heavy bottomed pan with a lid over a medium heat. Add the onion and carrot and cook for 5-6 minutes until softened.

2. Add the garlic, curry powder and fenugreek and cook for a further minute until fragrant.

3. Add the potatoes to the pan followed by the chicken stock and milk. Bring up to boiling and then turn down to a simmer and place the lid on top. Leave for 15-20 minutes until the potatoes have softened.

4. Blend the soup with a hand blender, leaving a few chunky pieces for texture.

5. Add the chicken and season with salt and black pepper to taste. Cook for a further 8-10 minutes to allow the chicken to warm up and soften in the chowder.

6. Mix through the chopped coriander and spoon into serving bowls before garnishing with the reserved coriander.

Pumpkin soup

SERVES: 4 | PREP TIME: 20 MINUTES | COOKING TIME: 30 MINUTES

INGREDIENTS

2 tbsp olive oil

25 g / 1 oz. butter

1 onion, diced

2 cloves of garlic, chopped

1 tsp turmeric

500 g / 1 lb 1 oz. pumpkin flesh, diced

250 ml / 8 ½ fl. oz / 1 cup chicken stock

100 ml / 3 ½ fl. oz / ½ cup double (heavy) cream

Salt and freshly ground black pepper

2 tbsp black sesame seeds

METHOD

1. In a large pan, heat the oil and butter over a medium heat. Add the onion and sweat with the lid on for 8-10 minutes until softened. Add the garlic and turmeric and cook for a further minute until fragrant.

2. Add the pumpkin and mix through to coat in the spiced onions. Pour in the stock and cover. Leave to simmer for 20 minutes.

3. Pour in the cream and blend using a hand blender. Season to taste.

4. Pour the soup into serving bowls and top with the sesame seeds to garnish.

Leek and potato soup

SERVES: 4 | PREP TIME: 10 MINUTES | COOKING TIME: 40 MINUTES

INGREDIENTS

60 g / 2 oz / ¼ cup butter

4 leeks, green ends discarded and finely sliced

2 floury potatoes, peeled and diced

2 sprigs thyme

850 ml / 1 ½ pints / 3 ½ cups chicken or vegetable stock

250 ml / 9 fl. oz / 1 cup milk

salt and white pepper

½ bunch chives, chopped

METHOD

1. In a large pan melt the butter and when foaming add the leeks. Cook gently over a low heat until soft and slithery.

2. Add the potatoes and thyme and cook for a couple of minutes, then add the stock and milk. Bring to a simmer and cook gently for 20–25 minutes, until the potatoes are soft.

3. Remove the thyme stalks and whizz in a blender until smooth.

4. Return to the heat and reheat, seasoning carefully. Serve with chives sprinkled on top.

Mushroom soup

SERVES: 4-6 | PREP TIME: 10 MINUTES | COOKING TIME: 40 MINUTES

INGREDIENTS

50 g / 1 ¾ oz / ¼ cup unsalted butter

1 onion, peeled and finely chopped

500 g / 1 lb / 2 cups flat or wild mushrooms, finely chopped

1 clove garlic, crushed

50 g / 1 ¾ oz / ¼ cup plain (all-purpose) flour

1 glass dry white wine or port

1 litre / 2 ¼ pints / 4 ¼ cups chicken or vegetable stock

100 ml / 3 ½ fl. oz / ½ cup double (heavy) cream

½ bunch parsley, chopped plus stalks

METHOD

1. Heat the butter in a large deep pan and sweat the onion without browning for 5–10 minutes or until softened.

2. Add the mushrooms and garlic and cook for a further 5 minutes.

3. Stir in the flour and cook until the flour has turned a biscuit colour.

4. Pour over the stock, add the parsley stalks and bring to the boil, stirring constantly. Reduce to a simmer and cook for 10–15 minutes. Remove from the heat.

5. Liquidize the soup in batches then return to the pan. Add seasoning and cream and reheat the soup gently without boiling.

Prawn and aioli shooters

MAKES: 9 | PREP TIME: 15 MINUTES

INGREDIENTS

1 egg yolk

1 tsp Dijon mustard

300 ml / 10 fl. oz / 1 ¼ cups rapeseed oil

1 clove of garlic, minced

1 lemon, juiced

A pinch of cayenne pepper

400 g / 14 oz. cooked king prawns

Salt and cracked black pepper

Flat leaf parsley leaves

METHOD

1. Whisk together the egg yolk and mustard, slowly adding the oil. Once a third of the oil has been added and mixture has thickened the oil can be added more quickly.

2. Crush the garlic in a pestle and mortar with a pinch of salt. Stir the garlic and lemon juice into the mayonnaise to make an aioli. Add the cayenne and seasoning.

3. Set aside 27 whole king prawns. Chop the remaining prawns and mix them through the aioli.

4. Place two prawns into shooter glasses and top with the prawn and aioli mixture. Finish with a whole prawn and parsley leaf.

Cook's Corner

Cook's Bible
Main meals

Toad in the hole

SERVES: 4 | PREP TIME: 35 MINUTES | COOKING TIME: 20 MINUTES

INGREDIENTS

300 ml / 10 fl. oz / 1 ¼ cups milk

4 eggs

250 g / 9 oz / 1 cup plain (all-purpose) flour

1 tbsp grain mustard

8 chipolata sausages

4 tbsp vegetable oil or beef dripping

METHOD

1. Preheat oven to 220°C (200°C fan) / 425F / gas 7.

2. Make the batter: whisk together the eggs and milk and leave to stand for 15 minutes.

3. Heat the oil in a roasting tin and brown the sausages on all sides.

4. Whisk the flour into the milk and eggs then the mustard, then pour into the hot tin around the sausages.

5. Cook in the oven for 20 minutes until golden and billowing. Serve with onion gravy.

Peking duck

SERVES: 4 | PREP TIME: 35 MINUTES | COOKING TIME: 30 MINUTES

INGREDIENTS

4 duck breasts

2 tbsp runny honey

2 tbsp rice vinegar

1 ½ tbsp soy sauce

1 tbsp Chinese 5 spice

1 tbsp soft dark brown sugar

METHOD

1. Place the duck on a wire rack skin side up and dry thoroughly with kitchen paper. Score the skins with a sharp knife.

2. Mix together the ingredients and brush the skin and leave to marinate for about 30 minutes.

3. Preheat the oven to 190°C (170°C fan) / 375F / gas 5.

4. Brush the duck all over with the sauce and transfer the wire rack to a roasting tin. Pour a cup of water into the bottom of the tin and roast/steam for 30 minutes until the duck is cooked through and the skin is crisp.

5. You can quickly grill the skin if it hasn't crisped up.

6. Serve with rice or pancakes.

69

Battered fish

SERVES: 4 | PREP TIME: 10 MINUTES | COOKING TIME: 20 MINUTES

INGREDIENTS

4 thick fillets white fish such as hake, haddock or cod

a little seasoned flour

225 g / 8 oz / 1 cup self-raising flour

300 ml / 10 fl. oz / 1 ½ cups cold lager

pinch of cayenne pepper

vegetable oil for deep-frying

METHOD

1. Dust the fish fillets in a little seasoned flour to help the batter stick.

2. Whisk the flour and lager together to make a batter the consistency of double cream.

3. Heat the oil to 180°C / 350F.

4. Dip the fish fillets in the batter, thoroughly coating both sides then cook two at a time for about 10 minutes until deep golden brown and crisp.

5. Keep warm in a low oven while you cook the remaining fish.

6. Serve with lemon wedges, chips and mushy peas.

Duck à l'orange

SERVES: 3-5 | PREP TIME: 5 MINUTES | COOKING TIME: 1 HOUR, 45 MINUTES

INGREDIENTS

1 duck, weighing about 2 ¾ kg / 6 lb

salt and pepper

FOR THE SAUCE:

100 g / 3 ½ oz / ½ cup caster (superfine) sugar

2 tbsp water

2 oranges, grated zest

250 ml / 9 fl. oz / 1 cup orange juice

1 tbsp marmalade

75 g / 2 ½ oz / ⅓ cup butter, chilled and cubed

METHOD

1. Preheat the oven to 220°C (200°C fan) / 450F / gas 7.

2. Prick the duck with a knife and place in a roasting tin. Season and roast for 20 minutes.

3. Reduce the heat to 180°C / 350F / gas 4 and cook for 1 hour. Remove from the pan, drain and rest the duck on a plate.

4. Make the sauce: set the sugar and water in a pan over a low heat and swirl until the sugar has melted. Do not stir. Allow to bubble up.

5. Once dark golden, remove from the heat and carefully add any duck juices, orange zest and juice. Return to the heat and simmer for 10–15 minutes until thickened. Stir in the marmalade then whisk in the butter a cube at a time until shiny. Season.

Mozzarella and tomato spaghetti

SERVES: 2 | PREP TIME: 10 MINUTES | COOKING TIME: 15 MINUTES

INGREDIENTS

120 g / 4 ¼ oz. spaghetti

75 g / 2 ½ oz. cherry tomatoes

2 tbsp olive oil

50 g / 1 ¾ oz. buffalo mozzarella, sliced

1 tbsp chives, chopped

METHOD

1. Preheat the oven to 180°C (160°C fan) / 350F / gas 4

2. Cook the pasta in a pan of salted boiling water as per the packed instructions, drain and return to the pan.

3. As the pasta cook, place the tomatoes onto a baking tray and drizzle with half the oil. Place into the oven and roast for 8-10 minutes until the skin has started to crack and blister.

4. Mix the baked tomatoes into the cooked spaghetti, adding the remaining oil and the sliced mozzarella. Season with salt and black pepper.

5. Add to serving plates and top with the chopped chives.

Winter vegetable pie

SERVES: 4-6 | PREP TIME: 20 MINUTES | COOKING TIME: 1 HOUR

INGREDIENTS

2 tbsp olive oil

2 onions, diced

300 g / 10 ½ oz. carrots, peeled and sliced

300 g / 10 ½ oz. parsnips, peeled and sliced

4 garlic cloves, sliced

250 g / 9 oz. chestnut mushrooms, sliced

2 sprigs of rosemary, leaves chopped

2 sprigs of thyme, leaves only

400 g / 14 oz. canned chopped tomatoes

250 ml / 8 ½ fl. oz / 1 cup vegetable stock

300 g / 10 ½ oz. puff pastry

1 egg, beaten

METHOD

1. Preheat the oven to 180°C (160°C fan) / 350F / gas 4. Heat the oil in a large casserole pan over a medium heat. Add the onions and cook for 5-6 minutes until softened.

2. Add the carrots, parsnips, garlic and mushrooms to the pan and cook for a further 5 minutes before mixing through the herbs. Add the tomatoes and stock and simmer uncovered for 20 minutes until the sauce has thickened and reduced. Add seasoning.

3. Pour the vegetable mixture into either individual or one large pie dish. Roll out the pastry and place over the top of the pie mixture. Cut a few holes in the pastry and brush the top with the beaten egg.

4. Bake in the oven for 30 minutes.

Chicken bulgur wheat salad

SERVES: 2 | PREP TIME: 15 MINUTES | COOKING TIME: 20 MINUTES

INGREDIENTS

50 ml / 1 ¾ fl. oz / ¼ cup olive oil

300 g / 10 ½ oz. chicken breast, sliced

Sea salt and cracked black pepper

100 g / 3 ½ oz. bulgur wheat

100 g / 3 ½ oz. mixed salad leaves

½ cucumber, sliced

75 g / 2 ½ oz. cherry tomatoes, halved

1 clove of garlic, minced

1 tsp Dijon mustard

1 tsp honey

1 lemon, juiced

METHOD

1. Heat 1 tbsp of the oil in a frying pan and fry the chicken for 12-15 minutes until browned and cooked through. Season with salt and black pepper whilst cooking.

2. Place the bulgur wheat into a saucepan half filled with boiling water. Cook for 8-10 minutes until tender, drain and set aside.

3. In a large mixing bowl combine the salad leaves, cucumber and cherry tomatoes.

4. Whisk together the remaining oil, garlic, mustard, honey and lemon to make a dressing. Season to taste.

5. Place the salad onto serving plates and top with the chicken and bulgur wheat before drizzling over the dressing.

Lamb tagine

SERVES: 4 | PREP TIME: 4 HOURS | COOKING TIME: 3 HOURS

INGREDIENTS

500 g / 18 oz lean diced lamb

2 tbsp ras-el-hanout spice mix

2 onions, peeled and sliced

4 cloves garlic, finely sliced

olive oil

2 x 400 g cans chopped tomatoes

500 ml / 1 pint / 2 cups chicken stock

100 g / 3 ½ oz / ½ cup dried apricots

50 g / 1 ¾ oz / ¼ cup dates

2 tbsp sultanas

2 tbsp honey

1 bunch coriander (cilantro), chopped

METHOD

1. Preheat the oven to 160°C (140°C fan) / 300F / gas 2. Add half the spice mix to the lamb. Marinade overnight or for at least 4 hours.

2. Heat 2 tablespoons of oil in a large casserole or tagine and cook the onions and garlic gently for at least 15 minutes until softened and sweet. Add the rest of the spice mix.

3. Add the lamb to the pan, then increase the heat a little to brown.

4. Add the tomatoes, stock and dried fruit with the honey and seasoning. Cover and bake in for 3 hours until the meat is very tender. Stir in the coriander.

5. If desired, serve packed into timbales and remove the moulds before serving.

Noodles with salmon, peas & broccoli

SERVES: 4 | PREP TIME: 10 MINUTES | COOKING TIME: 10 MINUTES

INGREDIENTS

4 nests dried noodles

1 head broccoli, cut into florets

100 g / 3 ½ oz / ½ cup frozen peas

1 tbsp groundnut oil

4 spring onions (scallions), finely chopped

1 cm (½ in) piece ginger, finely sliced

2 salmon fillets, boned and cut into strips

2 tbsp soy sauce

2 tbsp chilli (chili) sauce

1 tsp sesame oil

METHOD

1. Cook the noodles in boiling salted water according to packet instructions.

2. After 1 minute add the broccoli and peas.

3. Drain well.

4. Meanwhile heat the oil in a wok and add the spring onions and ginger.

5. Sauté for a few minutes, then add the salmon and cook until just pink.

6. Add the noodles and vegetables and pour in the sauces.

7. Toss well to coat, then serve drizzled with sesame oil.

Beef Wellington

SERVES: 6 | PREP TIME: 45 MINUTES | COOKING TIME: 20 MINUTES

INGREDIENTS

1 beef fillet, weighing 1 kg / 2 ¼ lb

3 tbsp olive oil

3 tbsp butter

250 g / 9 oz / 1 cup mushrooms

1 shallot, finely chopped

2 sprigs thyme leaves

75 ml / 2 ½ oz / ⅓ cup dry white wine

1 sheet ready rolled puff pastry

1 tbsp flour

2 egg yolks, beaten

TO SERVE:

750 g / 1 ⅓ lb / 3 cups new
potatoes, roasted

METHOD

1. Preheat oven to 220°C (200°C fan) / 450F / gas 7.

2. Drizzle the beef with oil and roast for 15 minutes. Place the mushrooms and shallot in a processor and process as finely as possible.

3. Heat the butter in a pan and dry the mushroom mixture with thyme leaves and a little seasoning until softened. Add the wine and cook until the wine has been absorbed.

4. Roll the pastry out and spoon the mushrooms over the pastry. Roll the pastry up, fully encasing the beef. Seal with egg yolk, then brush with the remaining egg.

5. Reduce the oven to 200°C (180°C fan) / 400F / gas 6 and roast for 20 minutes until puffed and golden.

77

Coq au vin

SERVES: 4 | PREP TIME: 20 MINUTES | COOKING TIME: 1 HOUR

INGREDIENTS

50 g / 1 ¾ oz / ¼ cup butter

6 rashers smoked streaky bacon or pancetta, diced

2 onions, peeled and finely sliced

3 cloves garlic, finely sliced

2 sprigs thyme

1 chicken, jointed

2 tbsp seasoned flour

300 g / 10 oz / 1 ¼ cups chestnut mushrooms, quartered

600 ml / 1 pint / 2 cups medium white wine, such as Riesling

300 ml / 10 fl. oz / 1 ½ cups double (heavy) cream

salt and pepper

2 tbsp parsley, chopped

squeeze of lemon juice

METHOD

1. Heat the butter in a casserole and fry the bacon until starting to brown.

2. Add the onion and garlic and cook until lightly gold. Add the thyme.

3. Using a slotted spoon, remove the bacon and onions from the pan to a bowl.

4. Add a little oil. Lightly dust the chicken joints with flour, shake off any excess and brown on all sides in the pan.

5. Add the mushrooms and cook until golden, then return the bacon and onions to the pan.

6. Pour over the wine, bubble up and cook gently for about 30 minutes until the chicken is cooked through.

7. Pour in the cream and parsley, season and add a little lemon juice. Heat until the cream starts to thicken, then serve.

Sweet and sour pork

SERVES: 4 | PREP TIME: 15 MINUTES | COOKING TIME: 20 MINUTES

INGREDIENTS

500 g / 1 lb pork loin, cubed

1 egg white

2 tsp cornflour

salt

1 tsp sesame oil

1 tbsp vegetable oil

1 carrot, peeled and cut into matchsticks

1 red pepper, deseeded and finely sliced

50 g / 1 ¾ oz / ¼ cup pineapple chunks

FOR THE SAUCE:

125 ml / 4 fl. oz / ½ cup pineapple juice

splash of dry sherry or rice wine

2 tbsp tomato ketchup

2 tbsp soy sauce

2 tbsp Chinese vinegar or red wine vinegar

METHOD

1. Slice the pork into strips.

2. Combine the egg white, cornflour, a pinch of salt and sesame oil in a bowl then thoroughly coat the pork strips in the mixture.

3. Heat the vegetable oil in a wok until smoking, then add the coated pork and stir-fry over a high heat until the pork is fully cooked.

4. Remove the pork from the pan and set aside. Discard the oil.

5. Heat the oil in the wok again and stir-fry the vegetables over a high heat for 4 minutes.

6. Mix together the sauce ingredients. Add the pork back to the pan with the sauce, bubble up and serve with white rice.

Sticky roast chicken thighs

SERVES: 2 | PREP TIME: 10 MINUTES | COOKING TIME: 45 MINUTES

INGREDIENTS

2 lemons, juiced

2 tbsp honey

1 tsp paprika

1 tsp chilli (chili) flakes

2 cloves of garlic, minced

1 tsp mustard

Sea salt and cracked black pepper

6 large chicken thighs

1 red chilli (chili) sliced

barbecue sauce to serve

METHOD

1. Preheat the oven to 200°C (180°C fan) / 400F / gas 6.

2. Mix the lemon, honey, paprika, chilli, garlic, mustard, salt and pepper to form a marinade.

3. Trim any of excess skin from the chicken before coating in the sauce. Leave to marinade for at least 30 minutes before cooking, longer if possible.

4. Place the chicken into a roasting pan and pour over the marinade. Roast in the oven for 45 minutes, basting a couple of times during cooking. The skin should be caramelised and crisp once ready.

5. Garnish with chopped chilli and alongside a barbecue sauce for dipping.

Roast potato salad

SERVES: 1 | PREP TIME: 10 MINUTES | COOKING TIME: 30 MINUTES

INGREDIENTS

1 large potato, peeled and cut into wedges

2 tbsp olive oil

1 tbsp sea salt

75 g / 2 ½ oz. mixed salad leaves

50 g / 1 ¾ oz. cherry tomatoes, halved

¼ red onion, sliced

25 g / 1 oz feta cheese, crumbled

Extra virgin olive oil to serve

METHOD

1. Preheat the oven to 220°C (200°C fan) / 425F / gas 7.

2. Add the potatoes to a baking tray and drizzle over the oil and salt. Turn the potatoes around in the oil and salt to coat all sides.

3. Bake the potato in the hot oven for around 30 minutes until golden and crisp.

4. Arrange the salad leave and tomatoes on a serving plate. Add the roast potato to the plate and scatter over the onion and feta cheese. Season with salt and black pepper and drizzle with olive oil.

Beef meatballs in tomato sauce

SERVES: 6 | PREP TIME: 40 MINUTES | COOKING TIME: 30 MINUTES

INGREDIENTS

400 g / 14 oz / 1 ½ cups minced beef

1 egg

2 tbsp parsley, chopped

1 clove garlic, crushed

½ lemon, grated zest

salt and pepper

1 thick slice of white bread, crusts removed soaked in 2 tbsp milk

3 tbsp olive oil

1 x 400 g can chopped tomatoes

400 ml / 14 fl. oz / 1 ½ cups beef stock

1 tsp sugar

METHOD

1. Place the meat in a large bowl with the egg, garlic, lemon zest and 1 tablespoon of parsley and season.

2. Mulch the bread in your fingers and crumble into the mix. Mix everything together with your hands to become smooth and sticky.

3. Roll into small walnut-sized balls with cold wet hands, place on a tray and chill for 30 minutes.

4. Heat the oil in a pan and fry the meatballs in batches until brown.

5. Add the tomatoes and stock, then add the sugar and season and bring to the boil. Lower the heat and simmer for about 20 minutes.

84

Spaghetti bolognese

SERVES: 4 | PREP TIME: 15 MINUTES | COOKING TIME: 40 MINUTES

INGREDIENTS

500 g / 1 lb / 2 cups spaghetti

3 tbsp olive oil

2 onions, peeled and finely chopped

2 cloves garlic, chopped

1 pack pancetta or bacon lardons

500 g / 1 lb / 2 cups minced beef

100 g / 3 ½ oz / ½ cup chicken livers, finely chopped

1 glass dry white wine

2 x 400 g can chopped tomatoes

4 tbsp double (heavy) cream

100 g / 3 ½ oz / ½ cup Parmesan, grated

1 bunch parsley, chopped

METHOD

1. Heat the oil in a pan and sweat the onion and garlic without browning. Add the pancetta and fry until the fat runs.

2. Add the mince and break it up with a wooden spoon, stirring frequently until browned. Add the chicken livers and cook until browned all over.

3. Season, then add the wine, bubble up, then add the tomatoes. Partially cover and simmer for 20 minutes.

4. Meanwhile cook the pasta in boiling salted water according to packet instructions. Drain and toss with a little oil.

5. Stir the cream and parsley through the sauce, then toss the pasta in the sauce.

Ratatouille

SERVES: 4 | PREP TIME: 10 MINUTES | COOKING TIME: 50 MINUTES

INGREDIENTS

4–6 tbsp olive oil

2 onions, peeled and finely sliced

2 aubergines (eggplants), cut in half lengthways and finely sliced

3 courgettes (zucchini), cut in half lengthways and finely sliced

2 cloves garlic, finely chopped

3 red peppers, seeded and cut into strips

1 x 400 g can chopped tomatoes

1 tsp coriander seeds, crushed

salt and pepper

handful fresh basil leaves

METHOD

1. Heat the oil in a pan and cook the onions until deep gold and sweet.

2. Add the aubergines and cook for 2 minutes, then add the courgettes and garlic and cook for 2 minutes, then add the peppers and cook for 5 minutes.

3. Add the tomatoes and coriander seeds and leave to simmer for at least 30 minutes over a very low heat, stirring occasionally, until the vegetables are very soft.

4. Season and sprinkle over the basil before serving.

Macaroni cheese

SERVES: 4 | PREP TIME: 15 MINUTES | COOKING TIME: 25 MINUTES

INGREDIENTS

2 tbsp butter

2 tbsp plain (all-purpose) flour

500 ml / 1 pint / 2 cups milk

1 bay leaf

1 tsp mustard powder

pinch of cayenne

grated nutmeg

150 g / 5 oz / ⅔ cup strong Cheddar cheese, grated

salt and pepper

320 g / 11 oz / 1 ¼ cups macaroni pasta

METHOD

1. Preheat the oven to 180°C (160°C fan) / 350F / gas 4. Melt the butter in a pan, then add the flour and stir to form a paste. Cook out for a couple of minutes, then gradually whisk in the milk to form a smooth sauce.

2. Stir in the seasonings and 2/3 of the cheese and simmer very gently for 10–15 minutes.

2. Cook the pasta in boiling salted water. Drain thoroughly, retaining a little of the water.

3. Tip the pasta into four individual ramekins and cover with the cheese sauce, adding a little of the cooking water to each to loosen.

4. Scatter over the remaining cheese and bake for 20–25 minutes until bubbling and golden.

Spinach & ricotta cannelloni

SERVES: 4 | PREP TIME: 35 MINUTES | COOKING TIME: 20 MINUTES

INGREDIENTS

12 cannelloni tubes or
12 sheets lasagne

FOR THE FILLING:
2 tbsp butter
olive oil
2 cloves garlic, chopped
¼ nutmeg, grated
1 kg / 2 lb / 4 ½ cups spinach leaves
400 g / 13 ½ oz / 1 ½ cups ricotta
2 tbsp Parmesan, grated
salt and pepper

FOR THE TOMATO SAUCE:
2 tbsp olive oil
1 clove garlic, chopped
2 x 400 g can chopped tomatoes
½ bunch basil, chopped

METHOD

1. Preheat the oven to 180°C (160°C fan) / 350F / gas 5.

2. Make the filling: heat the butter in a large pan with a little oil and cook the garlic for 2 minutes. Add the spinach and nutmeg and stir until wilted.

3. Spoon into a sieve and press down firmly with a wooden spoon to extract as much liquid as possible. Once done, finely chop the spinach and leave to cool in a bowl.

4. Stir in the ricotta, Parmesan and seasoning.

5. Spoon into the tubes or onto the lasagne sheets and roll up to make 12 cylinders, then lay in a greased baking dish.

6. Make the tomato sauce: heat the oil in a pan and add the garlic and tomatoes. Leave to simmer, topped up with ½ a can of water, for 10 minutes, then add the basil.

7. Spoon over the cannelloni and bake for around 15 minutes until bubbling.

Chicken Kiev

SERVES: 4 | PREP TIME: 10 MINUTES | COOKING TIME: 20 MINUTES

INGREDIENTS

4 chicken breasts, skinned

75 g / 2 ¾ oz / ⅓ cup plain
(all-purpose) flour

3 eggs, beaten

250 g / 9 oz / 1 cup breadcrumbs

4 tbsp vegetable oil

salt and pepper

FOR THE STUFFING:

225 g / 8 oz / 1 cup butter, softened

2–3 cloves garlic, crushed

½ bunch parsley, finely chopped

½ bunch tarragon, finely chopped

squeeze of lemon juice

METHOD

1. Using a sharp knife, cut a pocket in the side of each chicken breast.

2. Mix together the stuffing ingredients until well combined.

3. Use a teaspoon to stuff the pocket with the herb butter, then press the edges firmly together.

4. Place the flour, eggs and breadcrumbs on separate plates. Season the flour.

5. Dip each chicken breast into the flour, eggs then polenta, coating thoroughly each time.

6. Heat the oil then add the chicken breasts and cook, turning regularly for about 20 minutes until cooked through.

Cottage pie

SERVES: 4-6 | PREP TIME: 25 MINUTES | COOKING TIME: 35 MINUTES

INGREDIENTS

2 tbsp vegetable oil

450 g / 1 lb / 2 cups minced beef

1 onion, peeled and finely chopped

2 carrots, peeled and finely chopped

2 sticks celery, finely chopped

100 g / 3 ½ oz / ½ cup flat field mushrooms,
finely chopped

1 tbsp tomato purée

1 bay leaf

1 sprig rosemary

350 ml / 12 fl. oz / 1 ½ cups beef stock

salt and pepper

FOR THE TOPPING:

900 g / 2 lb / 3 ½ cups floury potatoes, peeled and
cut into chunks

100 g / 3 ½ oz / ½ cup butter

METHOD

1. Preheat the oven to 180°C (160°C fan) / 350F / gas 4.

2. Heat the oil in a large pan and briskly fry the lamb mince. Add the vegetables and sweat until soft.

3. Stir in the tomato purée and cook out for 2 minutes, before adding the herbs and pouring over the stock. Simmer until the stock has reduced and there is just a little liquid left in the bottom of the pan.

4. Meanwhile cook the potatoes in boiling salted water until tender to the point of a knife.

5. Drain thoroughly, then mash until completely smooth with the butter and season well.

6. Pour the lamb base into a baking dish, then spoon over the mashed potato. Run a fork down the length of the potato to create edges that will crisp in the oven.

7. Bake for 30 minutes until bubbling and golden.

Beef bourguignon

SERVES: 6 | PREP TIME: 15 MINUTES | COOKING TIME: 3 HOURS

INGREDIENTS

1 kg / 2 ¼ lb / 4 ¼ cups stewing beef, cubed

225 g / 7 ½ oz / 1 ½ cups baby carrots, washed and scrubbed

3 tbsp vegetable oil

1 onion, peeled and sliced

1 tbsp flour

400 ml / 14 fl. oz / 1 ½ cups red wine (preferably Burgundy)

2 cloves garlic, sliced

1 sprig thyme

1 bay leaf

12 pearl or button onions, peeled

225 g / 8 oz / 1 cup smoked streaky bacon, diced

200 g / 7 oz / ¾ cup chestnut mushrooms

salt and pepper

METHOD

1. Preheat the oven to 140°C (120°C fan) / 275F / gas 1.

2. Sear the beef in 1 tablespoon of oil in a casserole until brown all over. Remove with a slotted spoon.

3. Add the onion and cook until beginning to brown, then return the meat to the pan.

4. Stir in the flour and soak up the juices, then pour in the wine. Add the garlic and herbs, season, cover with a lid and cook for 2 hours.

5. Meanwhile fry the onions and bacon in a little oil, then add, with the mushrooms and carrots to the casserole and cook for 1 more hour.

6. Adjust the seasoning and serve.

Salmon with new potatoes and broccoli

SERVES: 2 | PREP TIME: 10 MINUTES | COOKING TIME: 25 MINUTES

INGREDIENTS

200 g / 7 oz. Jersey royal new potatoes

200 g / 7 oz. tenderstem broccoli

2 x 260 g / 9 oz. salmon fillets

1 tbsp olive oil

1 lemon, quartered

butter to serve

METHOD

1. Place the potatoes into a pan of boiling salted water and cook for 20-25 minutes until softened. Drain and return to the pan to keep warm.

2. Boil some salted water in a separate saucepan and add the broccoli. Cook for around 5 minutes until tender drain and return to the pan to keep warm.

3. Wash and pat the salmon fillets dry with kitchen paper and season the skin with plenty of salt.

4. Heat the oil in a non-stick frying pan over a medium high heat. Place the fish skin side down in the pan and fry for 3-5 minutes. Season the flesh side with salt and black pepper.

5. Turn the fish over and fry the other side for 2-3 minutes before squeezing over some lemon juice.

6. Place the cooked fish onto serving plates with the potatoes and broccoli. Place some butter on the potatoes and serve with lemon quarters.

Irish stew

SERVES: 4 | PREP TIME: 15 MINUTES | COOKING TIME: 6 HOURS

INGREDIENTS

55 ml / 2 fl. oz / ¼ cup sunflower oil

450 g / 1 lb / 3 cups lamb
shoulder, diced

300 g / 10 ½ oz / 2 cups new potatoes, peeled and
sliced

2 carrots, peeled and sliced

2 onions, chopped

1 tbsp juniper berries, lightly crushed

2–3 bay leaves

500 ml / 18 fl. oz / 2 cups lamb stock

salt and pepper

TO GARNISH:
1 tbsp curly leaf parsley leaves,
finely chopped

METHOD

1. Heat half of the oil in a large casserole dish
    set over a moderate heat until hot.

2. Season the lamb generously and seal in
    batches until golden brown in colour
    all over.

3. Transfer the sealed lamb to a slow cooker
    and reduce the heat under the casserole
    dish a little.

4. Add the remaining oil and sauté the onions
    and carrots for 4–5 minutes,
    stirring occasionally.

5. Add the bay leaves, potatoes, juniper berries,
    stock and a little seasoning and stir well.

6. Pour on top of the lamb in the slow cooker
    and stir thoroughly.

7. Cover and cook on a medium setting
    for 6 hours.

8. Adjust the seasoning to taste after 6 hours
    and ladle the stew into serving dishes.

9. Garnish with the chopped parsley
    before serving.

Seafood spaghetti

SERVES: 4 | PREP TIME: 10 MINUTES | COOKING TIME: 20 MINUTES

INGREDIENTS

350 g / 12 ¼ oz spaghetti

2 tbsp olive oil

1 onion, diced

1 clove of garlic, minced

1 tsp tomato purée

300 g / 10 ½ oz. mixed vegetables

400 g / 14 oz. mixed seafood selection

Salt and cracked black pepper

Flat leaf parsley to garnish

METHOD

1. Cook the spaghetti in of salted boiling water.

2. Heat the oil in a large pan over a medium heat. Add the onion and cook for 4-5 minutes until softened, add the garlic and fry for a further minute until fragrant.

3. Add the tomato purée to the pan followed by the mixed vegetables. Stir the vegetables through the onions and tomato to coat. Add some of the water from the pasta pan to loosen the sauce and cook for 8-10 minutes.

4. Add the seafood to the vegetables and cook for a further 5 minutes.

5. Add the drained spaghetti to the pan and stir through to coat the pasta in the sauce. Season to taste before adding to serving plates and topping with the parsley.

Chicken curry

SERVES: 4 | PREP TIME: 5 MINUTES | COOKING TIME: 45 MINUTES

INGREDIENTS

2 tbsp sunflower oil

1 onion, finely chopped

1 tbsp fresh root ginger, grated

3 cloves of garlic, crushed

8 skinless, boneless chicken thighs, cut into chunks

1 tbsp curry powder

400 g / 14 oz / 2 cups canned tomatoes, chopped

200 ml / 7 fl. oz / ¾ cup coconut milk

2 tbsp mango chutney

1 small bunch coriander, chopped

METHOD

1. Heat the oil in a large saucepan and fry the onion for 8 minutes stirring occasionally.

2. Add the ginger and garlic and stir-fry for 2 minutes.

3. Add the chicken and cook for 4 minutes, stirring occasionally, until it starts to colour on the outside, then sprinkle over the curry powder and continue to cook for 1 minute.

4. Add the chopped tomatoes, coconut milk and mango chutney and bring to a gentle simmer. If the sauce doesn't cover the chicken, add a little water.

5. Cook the curry for 30 minutes, stirring occasionally, until the chicken is tender and the sauce has thickened.

Sausages with onion gravy

SERVES: 4 | PREP TIME: 10 MINUTES | COOKING TIME: 35 MINUTES

INGREDIENTS

8 sausages

vegetable oil

2 tbsp butter

2 large onions, peeled and thickly sliced

2 sprigs thyme

½ tbsp flour

150 ml / 5 fl. oz / ⅔ cup Marsala or red wine

400 ml / 14 fl. oz / 1 ½ cups beef stock

salt and pepper

1 tbsp grain mustard

METHOD

1. Preheat the oven to 200°C (180°C fan) / 400F / gas 6.

2. Prick the sausages all over with a fork.

3. Drizzle the sausages with oil in a roasting tin and roast for 30 minutes until browned all over, turning occasionally.

4. Meanwhile heat the butter in a pan and cook the onions with thyme for 15–20 minutes, until deep gold and sweet.

5. Stir in the flour and cook out for 2 minutes, then stir in the wine and stock. Season and simmer for 20 minutes.

6. Stir in the grain mustard, then serve with the cooked sausages and some mashed potato.

Caramelized spare ribs

SERVES: 4 | PREP TIME: 4 HOURS | COOKING TIME: 3 HOURS

INGREDIENTS

2 tbsp runny honey

3 tbsp tomato ketchup

1 tbsp black treacle or molasses

2 star anise, lightly crushed

2 tsp English mustard

pinch of chilli (chili) flakes

2 tbsp olive oil

salt and pepper

METHOD

1. Mix the marinade ingredients to taste.

2. Coat the ribs thoroughly in the marinade and refrigerate for at least 4 hours.

3. The next day, preheat the oven to 150°C (130°C fan) / 300F / gas 2.

4. Remove the ribs from the marinade and place in a roasting tin, cover with foil and cook slowly for 2–3 hours until the meat falls from the bone. Baste with any leftover marinade every now and then.

5. To serve, heat a griddle pan until hot and lay the ribs on to caramelize the outside. Season.

103

Paella

SERVES: 4 | PREP TIME: 20 MINUTES | COOKING TIME: 30 MINUTES

INGREDIENTS

5 tbsp olive oil

1 onion, peeled and finely sliced

75 g / 2 ½ oz / ⅓ cup chorizo, diced

2 cloves garlic, finely chopped

1 celery stick, finely chopped

1 red pepper, seeded and sliced

300 g / 10 oz / 1 ¼ cups paella rice

2 chicken thighs, cubed

1 litre / 2 ¼ pints / 4 ¼ cups
chicken stock

a pinch of saffron threads

1 tsp paprika

4 ripe tomatoes, chopped

50 g / 1 ¾ oz / ¼ cup frozen peas

12 raw prawns (shrimp), shell on

24 mussels, cleaned

2 fillets chunky white fish, skinned, boned and cubed

1 lemon, juiced

salt and pepper

METHOD

1. Heat the olive oil in a large shallow pan and cook the onion, garlic and celery with the chorizo until the orange fat runs.

2. Add the pepper, cook for a further 5 minutes, then stir in the chicken and paella rice and coat thoroughly in the oil.

3. Stir the saffron into the stock then pour it over the rice. Add the paprika. Bring to a simmer and leave uncovered for 10 minutes.

4. Add the tomatoes, peas and seafood and cook for a further 8–10 minutes until everything is just cooked through and the mussels have opened.

5. Stir through the lemon juice, season well and serve.

Fresh gnocchi

SERVES: 4 | PREP TIME: 45 MINUTES | COOKING TIME: 5 MINUTES

INGREDIENTS

700 g / 24 oz floury potatoes, such as
Maris Piper

250 g / 9 oz / 1 ⅔ cups plain (all-purpose) flour

1 egg, beaten

salt

nutmeg

METHOD

1. Boil the potatoes whole and unpeeled in salted water for at least 25 minutes. Drain and mash thoroughly. Leave to cool.

2. Tip the potatoes into a bowl and work in the flour, egg, a pinch of salt and nutmeg until you have a smooth dough. Cut the dough in half and roll out to make 2 fat sausages.

3. Cut into pieces about 3 cm (1 ¼ in) long and press down gently with the tines of a fork to make the traditional indentations. Cool.

4. To cook the gnocchi, bring a large pan of salted water to the boil then add the gnocchi. When they float to the top, they are ready, so remove and drain on kitchen paper.

Tagliatelle carbonara

SERVES: 4 | PREP TIME: 5 MINUTES | COOKING TIME: 12 MINUTES

INGREDIENTS

500 g / 1 lb / 2 cups tagliatelle

2 tbsp butter

12 slices pancetta or smoked
streaky bacon, chopped

4 egg yolks

100 ml / 3 ½ fl. oz / ½ cup double
(heavy) cream

2 tbsp Parmesan, grated

METHOD

1. Cook the pasta in boiling salted water
   according to packet instructions.

2. Heat the butter in a pan and fry the pancetta
   until golden.

3. Whisk the egg yolks and Parmesan into
   the cream.

4. Drain the pasta, return to the pan and,
   working quickly, scrape the pancetta and
   butter into the pan and toss.

5. Toss off the heat with the egg and cream
   mixture then serve immediately.

Chilli con carne

SERVES: 4 | PREP TIME: 20 MINUTES | COOKING TIME: 2 HOURS 10 MINUTES

INGREDIENTS

2 tbsp vegetable oil

500 g / 1 lb / 2 full cups stewing beef, diced

1 onion, peeled and chopped

2 cloves garlic, finely chopped

1 tsp paprika

1 tsp ground cumin

1 tsp cinnamon

½–1 tsp cayenne pepper or ½ tsp dried chilli (chili) flakes

1 x 400 g can kidney beans

1 x 400 g can chopped tomatoes

300 ml / 10 fl. oz / 1 ¼ cups beef stock

20 g dark chocolate, finely chopped

TO SERVE:

1 lime, juiced

sour cream

rice

METHOD

1. Heat the oil in a large casserole and cook the beef until browned. Remove with a slotted spoon.

2. Add the onion and garlic and fry for a further 5 minutes until golden.

3. Add the spices and mix well, then pour over the kidney beans, tomatoes and stock, add the beef back in and bring to the boil.

4. Simmer over a low heat for at least 2 hours, stirring occasionally, until the chilli has thickened and reduced.

5. When the meat is falling apart, stir in the chocolate and season.

6. Serve with a squeeze of lime juice, sour cream and rice.

108

Beef stroganoff

SERVES: 4 | PREP TIME: 15 MINUTES | COOKING TIME: 20 MINUTES

INGREDIENTS

2 tbsp butter

1 onion, peeled and sliced

2 cloves garlic, finely sliced

400 g / 14 oz / 1 ½ cups mushrooms, sliced

500 g / 1 lb / 2 cups sirloin or rump steak,
thinly sliced

275 ml / 10 fl. oz / 1 cup sour cream

1 tbsp smoked paprika

TO GARNISH:

chopped cornichons

flat leaf parsley

METHOD

1. Fry the onions and garlic in the butter until
    golden and sweet then add the mushrooms.
    Cook until all the liquid has completely
    evaporated and season to taste. Remove
    from the pan with a slotted spoon.

2. Increase the heat and fry the beef quickly for
    2 minutes, then return the vegetables to the
    pan and pour in the sour cream and paprika.

3. Bubble up, adjust the seasoning and serve
    with the garnishes.

Pasties

MAKES: 6 | PREP TIME: 1 HOUR | COOKING TIME: 1 HOUR

INGREDIENTS

125 g / 4 ½ oz / ½ cup butter, frozen

125 g / 4 ½ oz / ½ cup lard, frozen

450 g / 1 lb oz / 3 cups plain (all purpose) flour

450 g / 1 lb / 3 cups beef skirt, finely chopped or coarsely minced

250 g / 9 oz / 2 cups floury potatoes, peeled and finely chopped

250 g / 9 oz / 2 cups swede, peeled and finely chopped

250 g / 9 oz / 2 cups onions, peeled and finely chopped

1 egg, beaten

METHOD

1. Grate the frozen butter and lard into the flour and add a pinch of salt. Toss well, then stir in just enough cold water to bring the pastry together into a pliable dough. Chill for 30 minutes.

2. Meanwhile, toss the beef with the potatoes, swede and onions and season generously.

3. Preheat the oven to 180°C (160°C fan) / 350F / gas 4.

4. Roll out the pastry on a lightly floured surface and cut out six 20 cm (8 in) circles. Divide the filling between the circles and brush the edges with water.

5. Fold the pastry in half to and press firmly to seal. Trim away excess pastry. Put the pasties on a large baking tray and brush with beaten egg. Bake for 1 hour.

Lamb hotpot

SERVES: 4 | PREP TIME: 25 MINUTES | COOKING TIME: 2 HOURS 15 MINUTES

INGREDIENTS

2 tbsp vegetable oil or dripping

1 kg / 2 ¼ lb / 4 ¼ cups neck of lamb, cut into chops

4 lambs' kidneys, cored and chopped small

4 onions, peeled and chopped

1 tbsp butter

1 tbsp flour

500 ml / 1 pint / 2 cups lamb stock or water

1 tbsp Worcestershire sauce

2 bay leaves

1 kg / 2 ¼ lb / 4 ¼ cups potatoes, peeled and cut into 2 cm slices

pickled red cabbage, to serve

METHOD

1. Preheat the oven to 170°C (150°C fan) / 325F / gas 3. Heat the fat in a large casserole and dry the meat in batches until browned. Add the kidney and cook alongside. Remove with a slotted spoon and set aside.

2. Add a little butter and onions and cook for a short while, then stir in the flour. Whisk in the stock and Worcestershire sauce and simmer. Add the meat and kidneys.

3. Add the herbs then top with slices of potato, seasoning the layers, arranging in an overlapping pattern.

4. Cover with a lid and bake for 1 ½ hours, then remove the lid and cook for a further 45 minutes to crisp up the potatoes.

Stuffed roast pheasant

SERVES: 2-4 | PREP TIME: 15 MINUTES | COOKING TIME: 30-40 MINUTES

INGREDIENTS

1 pheasant, cleaned and boned out
(ask your butcher)

FOR THE STUFFING:

250 g / 9 oz / 1 cup mild goat's cheese

2 tbsp parsley, finely chopped

1 tbsp thyme leaves

1 clove garlic, crushed

salt and pepper

METHOD

1. Put the onion in a bowl with the lemon juice
   and a pinch of salt. Stir well and leave to
   macerate for 15 minutes to soften the flavour
   and texture.

2. Shred the carrot with a julienne tool,
   mandolin or coarse grater and toss with
   the cabbages and onion.

3. Stir the mustard into the mayonnaise,
   then mix the dressing with the
   shredded vegetables.

Homemade burgers

SERVES: 4 | PREP TIME: 10 MINUTES | COOKING TIME: 25 MINUTES

INGREDIENTS

4 sirloin steaks, minced until coarsely ground
(ask your butcher)

1 tsp salt

1 tbsp grain mustard (optional)

black pepper

olive oil

4 slices Jarlsberg cheese

1 large tomato, thickly sliced

4 burger buns

METHOD

1. Season the meat well, mix well with
    the mustard if using and form into
    patties around 2 cm (1 in) thick.
    Refrigerate until needed.

2. Heat a griddle to very hot, then brush the
    burgers on each side with a little oil. Cook for
    3–4 minutes each side, then leave to rest for
    5–8 minutes wrapped in foil, the slices of
    cheese melting on top. Serve in buns topped
    with tomatoes, red onion and salad.

Roast chicken with vegetables

SERVES: 4-6 | PREP TIME: 20 MINUTES | COOKING TIME: 1 HOUR 30 MINUTES

INGREDIENTS

1 large free-range chicken

25 g / 1 oz. butter

1 lemon, quartered

1 bulb of garlic

2 tbsp olive oil

Sea salt and freshly ground black pepper

2 red onions, halved

4 Jersey royal potatoes

4-6 carrots, sliced lengthways

2 courgettes (zucchini), sliced

3-4 sprigs of rosemary

METHOD

1. Preheat the oven to 220°C (200°C fan) / 425F / gas 7. Wash the chicken inside and out, pat dry with kitchen paper.

2. Push the butter under the skin of the chicken and position over the thickest part of the breast meat. Place the lemon and half the bulb of garlic into the cavity of the chicken. Rub the oil over the chicken and season generously with salt and black pepper.

3. Place the chicken into a roasting tray and place into the hot oven and roast for 20 minutes.

4. Turn the heat down to 190°C (170°C fan) / 375F / gas 5 and remove the chicken from the oven. Baste with the juices before arranging the vegetables, remaining garlic and herbs. Use a spoon to mix the vegetables through the collected juices in the roasting pan.

5. Place back into the oven and roast for a further hour, or until the juices of the chicken run clear when pierced at the meatiest part of the bird.

6. Remove the chicken from the tray and cover in foil to rest for 10 minutes. Remove the vegetables and cover. Gravy can be made from the juices in the roasting pan.

Classic cheeseburger

SERVES: 2-4 | PREP TIME: 15 MINUTES | COOKING TIME: 10 MINUTES

INGREDIENTS

400 g / 14 oz. quality beef steak mince

1 tsp onion granules

1 tsp garlic powder

Sea salt and freshly ground black pepper

4 Cheddar cheese slices

100 g / 3 ½ oz. mayonnaise

1 tbsp ketchup

1 tsp sriracha sauce

½ lemon, juiced

4 burger buns

½ onion, sliced

50 g / 1 ¾ oz. salad leaves

1 tomato, sliced

METHOD

1. Place the steak mince, onion granules, garlic powder and a generous amount of salt and black pepper into a mixing bowl. Using your hands, bring the mixture together before dividing into four equal sized portions. Shape into round burger patties.

2. Heat a griddle pan or non-stick frying pan until hot. Place the patties into the pan and cook for 5 minutes without moving them. Flip the burgers over and cook for a further 5 minutes, placing the cheese slices on top of the burgers.

3. As the burgers cook mix the mayonnaise, ketchup, sriracha and lemon juice. Taste and season with salt and black pepper.

4. Cut the buns in half and place them under a grill, only toast the cut side of the buns.

5. Place the buns onto serving plates and top the bottom half with the onion and salad leaves. Place the burgers on top followed by the tomato and some of the burger sauce.

Easy Fish Pie

SERVES: 4 | PREP TIME: 15 MINUTES | COOKING TIME: 25 MINUTES

INGREDIENTS

900 g / 2 lb / 7 cups floury potatoes,
peeled and cubed

250 ml / 9 fl. oz / 1 cup whole milk

150 g / 5 ½ oz / 2/3 cup butter, cubed

450 g / 1 lb / 3 cups hot smoked salmon,
skinned and flaked

250 ml / 9 fl. oz / 1 cup crème fraîche

25 g / 1 oz / ¼ cup dried breadcrumbs

METHOD

1. Preheat the oven to 190°C (170°C fan) / 375F / gas 5.

2. Boil the potatoes in plenty of salted water for 12 minutes or until tender all the way through. Tip the potatoes into a colander and leave to drain.

3. Put the saucepan back on the heat and add the milk and butter. Heat until the milk starts to simmer then return the potatoes to the pan and mash until smooth.

4. While the potatoes are cooking, mix the salmon with the crème fraîche and spread it into an even layer in a baking dish.

5. Top with the mashed potato and swirl the top, then sprinkle with breadcrumbs.

6. Bake for 25 minutes or until piping hot all the way through. Serve immediately.

Persimmon and Gorgonzola salad

SERVES: 2 | PREP TIME: 10 MINUTES

INGREDIENTS

2 fuyu persimmon

100 g / 3 ½ oz. mixed leaf salad

75 g / 2 ½ oz. gorgonzola cheese, cubed

25 g / 1 oz. walnut halves

2 tbsp extra virgin olive oil

Salt and black pepper

METHOD

1. Ensure that you have the correct type of persimmon. Fuyu can be eaten firm and raw whereas hachiya needs to be very ripe and soft before being eaten.

2. Halve the persimmon and cut into slices. You can peel them if you like but the skin is edible.

3. Arrange the salad leaves across two serving plates and top with the persimmon, cheese and walnut halves.

4. Drizzle over the olive oil and season with salt and black pepper.

Paprika chicken thighs

SERVES: 4-6 | PREP TIME: 15 MINUTES | COOKING TIME: 45 MINUTES

INGREDIENTS

2 tbsp olive oil

1 tbsp paprika

1 tbsp honey

1 tsp cayenne pepper

1 lemon, juiced

6 large chicken thighs

4 cloves of garlic

2 sprigs of rosemary

2 red peppers, deseeded and diced

350 g / 12 ¼ oz. / 1 ¾ cups long grain rice

50 g / 1 ¾ oz. / ⅓ cup green olives

Salt and freshly ground black pepper

METHOD

1. Preheat the oven to 200°C (180°C fan) / 400F / gas 6.

2. Combine the oil, paprika, honey, cayenne and lemon juice in bowl. Season with salt and black pepper.

3. Pour the marinade over the chicken thighs and coat fully. Leave to marinade for at least 30 minutes.

4. Place the chicken in an ovenproof dish along with the garlic, rosemary and peppers. Roast in the oven for 40-45 minutes until the skin is crisp and chicken cooked through.

5. At the chicken is roasting, cook the rice as per the packet instructions.

6. To serve place the rice into a serving dish and arrange the chicken on top before scattering over the olives.

Beer battered fish and chips

SERVES: 1 | PREP TIME: 15 MINUTES | COOKING TIME: 30 MINUTES

INGREDIENTS

4 large Maris Piper potatoes, chipped

100 g / 3 ½ oz. mayonnaise

1 tbsp capers, chopped

2 gherkins, chopped

½ shallot, finely diced

1 lemon, juice

A handful of dill, finely chopped

A handful of flat leaf parsley, chopped

150 g / 5 ¼ oz. marrowfat peas

1 tsp sugar

75 g / 2 ½ oz. / ½ cup plain (all purpose) flour

1 tsp turmeric

A pinch of salt

125 ml / 4 ½ fl. oz / ½ cup Beer

1 white fish fillet, such as cod or haddock

Flour for dredging the fish

METHOD

1. Preheat a deep fat fryer to 160°C (140°C fan) / 325F / gas 3. Place the potatoes into the oil and gently cook for 20 minutes. Remove and leave in the frying basket to cool. Turn the heat on the fryer up to 190°C (170°C fan) / 375F / gas 5.

2. Make the tartar sauce by mixing the mayonnaise with the capers, gherkins, shallot, lemon juice and herbs.

3. Place the peas into a saucepan with the sugar and pour in enough water to just cover the peas. Cover and cook gently for 25-30 minutes and season to taste.

4. Combine the flour, turmeric and salt in a mixing bowl. Pour in the beer and whisk together until smooth.

5. Dip the fish in the flour until fully coated, then dip into the batter and gently drop into the hot oil. Leave to fry for 8-10 minutes. Remove and keep warm in the oven.

6. Return the chips to the fryer and cook for 2-3 minutes until crisp and golden. Place onto kitchen paper to drain and then season with salt and black pepper.

7. Serve plate with lemon wedges.

Cook's Corner

Cook's Bible

Desserts

Chocolate torte

SERVES: 8-10 | PREP TIME: 25 MINUTES | COOKING TIME: 2 HOURS

INGREDIENTS

250 g / 9 oz dark chocolate

2 tbsp golden syrup

568 ml / 19 ¼ fl. oz / 2 ⅓ cups double (heavy) cream

1 tsp cinnamon

175 g / 6 oz digestive biscuits

100 g / 3 ½ oz / ½ cup unsalted butter, melted

1 tbsp cocoa powder, plus more for dusting

50 g / 1 ¾ oz / 1/3 cup blueberries

METHOD

1. Break the chocolate into pieces in a heatproof bowl with the golden syrup. Place over a pan of boiling water, ensuring that the bowl is not touching the water. Gently heat until the chocolate has melted, remove from the heat and stir through a quarter of the cream until combined. Set aside to cool.

2. Whisk together the remaining cream with the cinnamon until it has thickened but is not whipped, it should have a slow wobble. Fold the chocolate into the cream mixture until combined. This may take a bit of time so be patient and do not whip quickly.

3. Prepare a 18cm springform cake tin by lining the base with some cling film.

4. Break up the biscuits in a bag or blender. Mix with the butter and cocoa powder to form a thick biscuit base. Press this into the base the prepared cake tin.

5. Pour the chocolate truffle mixture into the cake tin and level to a smooth finish.

6. Place into the refrigerator for at least 2 hours to set or overnight if you would prefer.

7. When ready to serve, gently heat the edges of the cake tin before releasing the spring mechanism. Slide onto a serving plate and dust with cocoa before topping with the blueberries.

Chocolate and yogurt parfaits

SERVES: 4 | PREP TIME: 10 MINUTES | CHILLING TIME: 2 HOURS

INGREDIENTS

900 g / 2 lb 10 oz Greek yogurt

250 ml / 8 ½ fl. oz / 1 cup double (heavy) cream

2 tbsp honey

1 tsp vanilla extract

1 tbsp ground pink peppercorns

25 g / 1 oz / ¼ cup cocoa powder, plus more for dusting

METHOD

1. Place the yogurt, cream, honey, vanilla and peppercorns into large mixing bowl and whisk together until fully combined and thickened in texture. The mixture should be silky smooth.

2. Place a third of the mixture into a separate bowl and whisk in the cocoa powder until fully combined.

3. Spoon the chocolate mixture into the bottom of serving glasses before topping with the plain yogurt mixture.

4. Place into the refrigerator to chill and set for at least 2 hours or overnight if preferred. Before serving dust with cocoa powder.

Poached pears

SERVES: 2 | PREP TIME: 10 MINUTES | COOKING TIME: 20 MINUTES

INGREDIENTS

2 tbsp honey

100 g / 3 ½ oz / ½ cup caster (superfine) sugar

2 lemons, juice and zest

400 ml / 13 ½ fl. oz / 1⅔ cups water

1 cinnamon stick

2 ripe pears, peeled

100 ml / 3 ½ fl. oz / ½ cup whipped cream

25 g / 1 oz / ¼ cup chopped nuts

METHOD

1. Place the honey, sugar, lemon, water and cinnamon into a saucepan that is just large enough to hold the pears. Gently heat and mix until the sugar has melted and the liquid has formed a syrup.

2. Place the pears into the syrup and leave to poach for around 12-15 minutes until softened. Carefully remove the pears from the pan and cut in half.

3. Place the halved pears onto serving plates and spoon over some of the cooking syrup. Place some whipped cream onto the pears and sprinkle over the chopped nuts.

Spiced stewed apples

SERVES: 2 | PREP TIME: 10 MINUTES | COOKING TIME: 10 MINUTES

INGREDIENTS

300 g / 10 ½ oz. baking apples

100 ml / 3 ½ fl. oz / ½ cup water

50 g / 1 ¾ oz. / ¼ cup caster (superfine) sugar

1 tsp cinnamon

1 tsp nutmeg

1 lemon, juice

200 g / 7 oz. natural yogurt

Apple slices to garnish

METHOD

1. Peel and core the apples before cutting them into dice sized cubes.

2. Add the apples, water and sugar to a saucepan and gently heat for 8-10 minutes until the apples start to break down.

3. Stir in the cinnamon, nutmeg and lemon juice and taste to check sweetness, add more sugar if desired.

4. Spoon the stewed apples into serving bowls and add some yoghurt and apple slices to garnish.

Black cherry crumble

SERVES: 2 | PREP TIME: 20 MINUTES | COOKING TIME: 45 MINUTES

INGREDIENTS

100 g / 3 ½ oz. / ⅔ cup wholemeal flour

50 g / 1 ¾ oz. / ¼ cup butter

100 g / 3 ½ oz. / ½ cup caster (superfine) sugar

400 g / 14 oz. black cherries in kirsch

2 tbsp demerara sugar

METHOD

1. Preheat the oven to 180°C (160°C fan) / 350F / gas 4. Place the flour, butter and half the sugar into a mixing bowl. Rub together with your fingertips until you have a breadcrumb like consistency. Place onto a baking tray and bake in the oven for 12-15 minutes.

2. Mix the remaining sugar with the cherries including the liquid from the jar. Warm in a saucepan until the sugar has melted.

3. Divide the cherries between two ovenproof dishes and top with the crumble mixture. Sprinkle over the sugar before placing onto a baking tray and baking in the oven for 30 minutes until golden and the cherry mixture is bubbling through the topping.

Blueberry muffins

MAKES: 12 | PREP TIME: 25 MINUTES | COOKING TIME: 18 MINUTES

INGREDIENTS

1 large egg

125 ml / 4 ½ fl. oz / ½ cup sunflower oil

125 ml / 4 ½ fl. oz / ½ cup soya milk

375 g / 12 ½ oz / 2 ½ cups self-raising flour, sifted

1 tsp baking powder

200 g / 7 oz / ¾ cup caster (superfine) sugar

150 g / 5 oz / 1 cup blueberries

METHOD

1. Preheat the oven to 180°C (160°C fan) / 350F / gas 4 and line a 12-hole muffin tin with paper cases.

2. Beat the egg in a jug with the oil and soya milk until well mixed.

3. Mix the flour, baking powder, sugar and blueberries in a bowl, then pour in the egg mixture and stir just enough to combine.

4. Divide the mixture between the cases, then bake in the oven for 18 minutes. Test with a wooden toothpick, if it comes out clean, the cakes are done. If not, test again in 5 minutes.

5. Transfer the cakes to a wire rack and leave to cool completely before serving.

Mocha muffins

MAKES: 12 | PREP TIME: 10 MINUTES | COOKING TIME: 20 MINUTES

INGREDIENTS

200 g / 7 oz. / ¾ cup caster (superfine) sugar

300 g / 10 ½ oz. / 2 cups self-raising flour

50 g / 1 ¾ oz. / 1 ¾ oz. / ¼ cup cocoa,
plus more to dust

250 ml / 8 ½ fl. oz / 1 cup milk

60 g / 2 oz. / ¼ cup unsalted butter, melted

1 tbsp espresso powder

2 large free-range eggs, beaten

METHOD

1. Preheat the oven to 200°C (180°C fan) / 400F / gas 6 and lightly grease a muffin tin.

2. Mix the sugar, flour and cocoa in a large mixing bowl.

3. In a separate bowl, whisk together the milk, butter, espresso powder and eggs.

4. Make a well in the centre of the dry ingredients, pour in the wet and mix just enough to combine.

5. Spoon the mixture into the prepared muffin tin. Bake in the oven for 20 minutes until risen and a skewer inserted into the centre comes out clean. Remove to cool completely.

Strawberry pavlova

SERVES: 6 | PREP TIME: 30 MINUTES | COOKING TIME: 1 HOUR

INGREDIENTS

4 large egg whites

200 g / 7 oz / ¾ cup caster (superfine) sugar

1 tsp cornflour (cornstarch)

2 tsp raspberry vinegar

250 ml / 9 fl. oz / 1 cup thick soya yoghurt

2 tbsp icing (confectioner's) sugar

½ tsp vanilla extract

250 g / 8 oz / 1 cup strawberries

METHOD

1. Preheat the oven to 140°C (120°C fan) / 275F / gas 1 and oil and line a baking tray with greaseproof paper.

2. Whisk the egg whites until stiff, then gradually whisk in half the sugar until the mixture is very shiny. Stir the cornflour into the vinegar, then fold it in with the remaining sugar. Spoon the mixture onto the baking tray and spread it into a circle with a palette knife.

3. Bake the meringue for 1 hour or until crisp on the outside, but still a bit chewy in the middle. Turn off the oven and leave the meringue to cool completely inside.

4. Mix the yoghurt with the icing sugar and vanilla extract, then spoon it on top of the meringue.

5. Carefully remove the leaves from the strawberries and set to one side. Cut half of the strawberries into quarters, leaving the rest whole, then arrange on top of the pavlova. Garnish with the strawberry leaves and serve immediately.

Watermelon sorbet

SERVES: 6-8 | PREP TIME: 20 MINUTES | CHILLING TIME: 4 HOURS

INGREDIENTS

200 g / 7 oz / ¾ cup caster (superfine) sugar

2 limes, juiced

200 ml / 7 fl. oz / ¾ cup water

1 watermelon

METHOD

1. Heat the sugar, lime juice and water over a medium heat in a saucepan. Stir continuously until the sugar has dissolved and you have a syrup. Remove from the heat and set aside to cool.

2. Peel the watermelon and cut into cubes removing the seeds.

3. Place the watermelon into a blender and blend to a smooth pulp.

4. Stir the cooled syrup through the blended watermelon before placing into an ice cream maker and processing as per the manufacturers guidelines.

5. Alternatively, place into a shallow metal container and place into the freezer. Leave for 30 minutes until ice crystals have formed at the edges. Move into the centre and return to the freezer. Repeat this process every 20 minutes until completely frozen.

6. Place into an airtight container and freeze for 4 hours or overnight.

7. Serve garnished with lime wedges and mint sprigs as desired.

139

Cranberry loaf cake

MAKES: 1 LOAF | PREP TIME: 15 MINUTES | COOKING TIME: 45 MINUTES

INGREDIENTS

225 g / 8 oz / 1 ½ cups self-raising flour

110 g / 3 ¾ oz / ½ cup unsalted butter

110 g / 3 ¾ oz / ½ cup caster (superfine) sugar

1 egg, beaten

75 ml / 2 ½ fl. oz / ⅓ cup milk

1 tsp vanilla extract

150 g / 5 ¼ oz / 1 cup fresh cranberries

1 orange, zest and juice

250 g / 9 oz / 2 ½ cups icing (confectioners') sugar

METHOD

1. Preheat the oven to 200°C (180°C fan) / 400F / gas 6 and line a loaf tin with greaseproof paper or a loaf cake case

2. Place the flour, butter and sugar into a blender and blend until you achieve a breadcrumb like consistency, add to a mixing bowl.

3. Combine the egg, milk and vanilla extract in a jug and whisk. Pour into the mixing bowl and stir with a wooden spoon until you have a smooth batter. Fold through the cranberries and half of the orange zest.

4. Pour into the prepared tin and bake in the oven for approximately 45 minutes or until a skewer inserted into the centre comes out clean. Remove from the oven to cool completely.

5. Mix the icing sugar with enough of the orange juice to make a smooth icing. Pour over the cooled cake and sprinkle over the remaining orange zest, leave to set.

Blueberry ice cream

SERVES: 4-6 | PREP TIME: 30 MINUTES | FREEZING TIME: 4 HOURS

INGREDIENTS

1 lemon, juice and zest

150 g / 5 ¼ oz. / ⅔ cup caster (superfine) sugar

150 g / 5 ¼ oz. / 1 cup blueberries, plus more to serve

500 ml / 17 fl. oz / 2 cups double (heavy) cream

METHOD

1. Combine the lemon, caster sugar and blueberries in a saucepan and heat gently until the sugar has dissolved and the blueberries are beginning to break down.

2. Place into a blender and blend until smooth.

3. Whip the cream until thickened and just about holding its shape. Fold the blueberries purée through the cream until combined.

4. Place into a solid container and freezer for 1 hour. Remove and whisk the mixture together and place back into the freezer. Repeat this process every hour until the mixture is smooth, place back into the freezer until firm, ideally overnight.

Eton mess

SERVES: 4 | PREP TIME: 20 MINUTES | COOKING TIME: 1 HOUR

INGREDIENTS

175 g / 6 oz / ¾ cup caster (superfine) sugar

3 egg whites

500 g / 1 lb / 2 cups raspberries,

1 tbsp icing (confectioner's) sugar

500 ml / 1 pint / 2 cups double (heavy) cream

1 tsp vanilla extract

METHOD

1. Preheat the oven to 150°C (130°C fan) / 300F / gas 2. Whisk the egg whites to soft peaks, then whisk in the sugar a little at a time, beating each addition in thoroughly, until thick and glossy.

2. Spoon onto lined baking trays and bake for 1 hour. Turn the oven off and leave until completely cold.

3. Purée half the raspberries with the icing sugar until smooth.

4. Whisk the cream to soft peaks, whisking in the vanilla as you go.

5. Break up the meringues and layer into individual serving dishes, spooning over a little purée, then adding raspberries and cream. Top with a raspberry and serve immediately.

143

Bakewell tart

SERVES: 8 | PREP TIME: 1 HOUR 40 MINUTES | COOKING TIME: 45 MINUTES

INGREDIENTS

110 g / 4 oz / ½ cup butter,
cubed and chilled

225 g / 8 oz / 1 ½ cups plain
(all purpose) flour

110 g / 4 oz / ½ cup raspberry jam (jelly)

200 g / 7 oz / 2 cups icing (confectioner's) sugar

1 tbsp unsweetened cocoa powder

FOR THE FRANGIPANE:

55 g / 2 oz / ½ cup ground almonds

55 g / 2 oz / ¼ cup caster
(superfine) sugar

55 g / 2 oz / ¼ cup butter, softened

1 large egg

1 tsp almond essence

METHOD

1. Rub the butter into the flour. Add just enough cold water to bind the mixture together into a dough.

2. Roll out the pastry on a floured surface and use it to line a 23 cm (9 in) round tart case. Leave the pastry to chill in the fridge for 30 minutes.

3. Preheat the oven to 200°C (180°C fan) / 400F / gas 6. Line the pastry case with cling film, fill it with baking beans, then bake for 15 minutes.

4. For frangipane, combine all the ingredients in a bowl and whisk until smooth.

5. When the pastry case is ready, remove the cling film and baking beans. Spread the base with jam. Top with the frangipane mixture and bake for 30 minutes. Leave to cool.

6. Sieve 150 g of icing sugar into a bowl and stir in warm water, 1 teaspoon at a time, to make a thick icing. Put the rest in a different bowl with the cocoa and repeat to make the chocolate icing.

7. Spread the plain icing over the tart in an even layer. Put the chocolate icing in a small piping bag and pipe parallel lines across the top. Drag a toothpick across the chocolate lines to feather.

Banoffee pie

SERVES: 6-8 | PREP TIME: 2-3 HOURS

INGREDIENTS

biscuits, crushed

200 g / 7 oz / ⅔ cup butter, melted

2 tins of condensed milk

500 ml / 1 pint / 2 cups double
(heavy) cream

2–3 ripe bananas

1 tbsp dark chocolate, grated

METHOD

1. Combine the biscuits and butter in a bowl then press into the bottom of a springform tin. Refrigerate.

2. Cover the condensed milk tins completely in boiling water and boil for 2 hours. Make sure they are covered at all times, topping up if necessary otherwise they will explode.

3. Remove from the water and leave to cool. Open the tins and scoop out the toffee.

4. Whizz the bananas with a spoonful of toffee in a food processor until smooth. Whisk the cream to soft peak then fold the banana mixture in until combined.

5. Spread half the banana cream over the biscuit base, then smooth over a layer of toffee, using a palette knife to even it out. Repeat, leaving a small amount of banana cream for piping.

6. Pipe rosettes of banana cream onto the top of the toffee, then decorate with grated chocolate. Refrigerate.

Bread and butter pudding

SERVES: 4-6 | PREP TIME: 15 MINUTES | COOKING TIME: 30-40 MINUTES

INGREDIENTS

8 thick slices white bread,
thickly buttered

50 g / 1 ¾ oz / ¼ cup sultanas,
soaked in a little brandy

300 ml / 10 fl. oz / 1 ¼ cups milk

60 ml / 3 fl. oz / ¼ cup double
(heavy) cream

50 g / 1 ¾ oz / ¼ cup caster
(superfine) sugar

3 eggs

freshly grated nutmeg

1 baking dish liberally buttered

METHOD

1. Preheat the oven to 180°C (160°C fan) / 350F /
gas 5.

2. Cut each slice of bread into two triangles and
arrange a layer in the base of the baking
dish. Sprinkle with the soaked sultanas and
add another layer of bread triangles.

3. Whisk together the milk, cream, sugar and
eggs until well combined, then pour over the
bread layers. Push the bread down into the
custard to soak
it thoroughly. The custard should just reach
the top of the bread – if it doesn't add a little
more milk and/or cream.

4. Grate over the nutmeg and bake in the oven
for 30–40 minutes until set and golden.

Chocolate fudge cake

SERVES: 8-10 | PREP TIME: 30 MINUTES | COOKING TIME: 30 MINUTES

INGREDIENTS

120 g / 4 oz / ½ cup self-raising flour

1 tsp baking powder

120 g / 4 oz / ½ cup butter, softened

120 g / 4 oz / ½ cup caster
(superfine) sugar

2 eggs

1 ½ tbsp cocoa powder

FOR THE FILLING AND ICING:

75 g / 2 ½ oz / ⅓ cup granulated sugar

75 ml / 2 ½ oz / ⅓ cup evaporated milk

120 g / 4 oz / ½ cup dark
chocolate, chopped

40 g butter, softened

25 g chocolate, shaved

METHOD

1. Preheat the oven to 170°C (150°C fan) / 325F / gas 3. Grease two 17 cm (7 in) cake tins.

2. Sieve the flour and baking powder into a large bowl, then add the other ingredients.

3. Divide the mixture equally between the two cake tins and cook for 30 minutes. Remove from the tins and cool on a wire rack.

4. Make the icing: combine the sugar and evaporated milk in a pan and stir to dissolve the sugar. Bring to the boil and simmer for 5 minutes, then stir in the chocolate and butter. Chill for at least 1 hour until it has thickened and is spreadable.

5. Use the icing to sandwich the cakes together, then smooth the remainder over the top and sides with a palette knife. Decorate with chocolate shavings.

149

Tiramisu

SERVES: 4 | PREP TIME: 25 MINUTES

INGREDIENTS

600 ml / 1 pint / 2 cups double (heavy) cream

250 g / 9 oz / 1 cup mascarpone

3 tbsp Marsala dolce

5 tbsp caster (superfine) sugar

300 ml / 10 fl. oz / 1 ¼ cups strong coffee

2 tbsp coffee liqueur (optional)

175 g / 6 oz sponge fingers (ladyfingers)

25 g dark chocolate, grated

3 tsp cocoa powder

chocolate shards, to decorate

METHOD

1. Place the cream, mascarpone, Marsala and sugar in a bowl and whisk until combined and thick.

2. Divide the coffee (and liqueur if using) between four dessert glasses and soak the sponge fingers in it.

3. Spoon over half the mascarpone mixture, then grate over half of the chocolate. Repeat until all the ingredients are used up.

4. Chill in the refrigerator for 3 hours.

5. Dust with cocoa powder and add chocolate shards to serve.

Chocolate truffles

MAKES: 40 | PREP TIME: 10 MINUTES | COOKING TIME: 10 MINUTES

INGREDIENTS

300 g / 10 ½ oz dark chocolate

300 ml / 10 fl. oz / 1 ¼ cups double (heavy) cream

1 tsp vanilla extract

1 tbsp unsalted butter

2 tbsp rum or brandy (optional)

A pinch of salt

Cocoa powder for dusting

50 g / 1 ¾ oz / ½ cup desiccated coconut

METHOD

1. Break the chocolate up into smaller pieces in a heatproof bowl. Heat the cream and vanilla in a saucepan until hot but not boiling, stir through the butter until melted.

2. Pour the hot cream over the chocolate and mix until the chocolate has melted. Mix through the salt and alcohol if using.

3. Place into the refrigerator for 1-2 hours until set.

4. Place the cocoa onto a plate and the coconut onto a separate plate. Remove the truffle mixture from the refrigerator and shape into balls using a spoon. Roll in either the cocoa or coconut as preferred before serving.

5. Keep in the refrigerator until ready to serve, these will keep for up to three days.

Vanilla ice cream

SERVES: 4-6 | PREP TIME: 30 MINUTES | FREEZING TIME: 4 HOURS

INGREDIENTS

4 egg yolks

200 g / 7 oz / ¾ cup caster (superfine) sugar

2 vanilla pod

500 ml / 17 fl. oz / 2 cups double (heavy) cream

METHOD

1. Whisk the egg yolks and sugar together until pale and creamy.

2. Halve the vanilla pods and scrape out the seeds.

3. Place the vanilla pods and cream into a saucepan and gently heat until just starting to bubble. Remove the vanilla pods from the cream and slowly pour over the egg yolks whilst whisking continuously.

4. Pour through a sieve back into the saucepan and add the vanilla seeds to the pan. Cover and leave to cool completely.

5. Pour the cooled mixture into a solid container and place into the freezer for 4 hours or overnight until frozen solid.

Rice pudding

SERVES: 4 | PREP TIME: 10 MINUTES | COOKING TIME: 2 HOURS 10 MINUTES

INGREDIENTS

3 tbsp butter, melted

60 g / 2 oz / ¼ cup pudding rice

30 g caster (superfine) sugar

1 tsp vanilla extract

500 ml / 1 pint / 2 cups full fat milk

fresh nutmeg

METHOD

1. Preheat the oven to 150°C (130°C fan) / 300F / gas 2.

2. Use half the butter to grease a baking dish.

3. Add the rice, sugar and vanilla extract, then pour over the milk.

4. Top with the remaining melted butter and grate over a little nutmeg.

5. Bake very gently for about 2 hours, stirring every 30 minutes until the milk is absorbed and the rice creamy.

Raspberry fool

SERVES: 4 | PREP TIME: 10 MINUTES

INGREDIENTS

300 g / 10 oz / 1 ¼ cups raspberries

150 ml / 5 fl. oz / ⅔ cup double (heavy) cream

125 ml / 4 fl. oz / ½ cup Greek natural yogurt

1 tbsp icing (confectioner's) sugar

a handful of mint sprigs

METHOD

1. Tip the raspberries into a bowl and lightly crush with a fork so that it is a mixture of liquid and fruit. This will give the fool a more interesting texture.

2. Lightly whip the cream to soft peaks, then fold in the yogurt.

3. Fold the raspberries through to make a ripple effect.

4. Serve in small dessert bowls or glasses, topped with a mint sprig.

Vanilla fudge

MAKES: 36 | PREP TIME: 45 MINUTES | SETTING TIME: 45 MINUTES

INGREDIENTS

300 ml / 10 fl. oz / 1 ¼ cups milk

350 g / 12 oz / 1 ½ cups caster (superfine) sugar

100 g / 3 ½ oz / ½ cup butter

1 tsp vanilla extract

METHOD

1. Lightly grease a 17 cm (7 in) cake tin or roasting tin. Place the ingredients, except the vanilla in a saucepan and heat slowly, stirring constantly, until the sugar has dissolved and the butter has melted.

2. Boil for around 15–20 minutes, stirring constantly, until the mixture reaches (115°C) or until a small amount of mixture dropped into a glass of cold water will form a soft ball that you can pick up on the end of a teaspoon. Remove from the heat, stir in the vanilla and leave to cool for 5 minutes.

3. Using a wooden spoon, beat the mixture until it thickens and the shine disappears.

4. Pour into the tin and set at room temperature for at least 45 minutes. Once set, cut into squares and serve.

Carrot cake

SERVES: 4 | PREP TIME: 20 MINUTES | COOKING TIME: 1HOUR, 30 MINUTES

INGREDIENTS

300 g / 10 oz / 1 ¼ cups plain (all-purpose) flour

1 tsp ground cinnamon

1 tsp baking powder

½ tsp bicarbonate of soda

200 g / 7 oz / ¾ cup soft dark brown sugar

4 eggs

250 ml / 9 fl. oz / 1 cup vegetable oil

zest of 2 oranges

zest of ½ lemon

200 g / 7 oz / ¾ cup grated carrots

125 g / 4 oz / ½ cup butter, softened

2 tbsp icing (confectioner's) sugar

250 g / 9 oz / 1 cup cream cheese

METHOD

1. Preheat the oven to 150°C (130°C fan) / 300F / gas 2. Grease and line a 20 cm (8 in) cake tin.

2. Sieve the flour into a bowl with cinnamon, baking powder and bicarbonate of soda, then stir in the sugar.

3. Beat the eggs with the oil and fold into the flour with the carrots and orange zest.

4. Spoon into the cake tin and bake for around 1 ½ hours until an inserted skewer comes out clean. Leave to cool.

5. Beat the butter and sugar together until pale, then beat in the cream cheese and lemon zest. Chill until spreadable and cover the cake using a palette knife to smooth.

Fresh fruit tart

SERVES: 6-8 | PREP TIME: 20 MINUTES | COOKING TIME: 15 MINUTES

INGREDIENTS

150 g / 5 ¼ oz / 1 cup plain (all purpose) flour

150 g / 5 ¼ oz. / ⅔ cup butter

125 g / 4 ¼ oz / ½ cup caster (superfine) sugar

1 free-range egg, whole

500 ml / 17 fl. oz / 2 cups double (heavy) cream

1 lemon, juiced

50 g / 1 ¾ oz strawberries, sliced

2 nectarines, segments only

50 g / 1 ¾ oz / ⅓ cup blueberries

mint leaves to garnish

METHOD

1. Preheat the oven to 200°C (180°C fan) / 400F / gas 6. Lightly grease a fluted tart tin.

2. In a bowl mix the flour, butter and half the sugar. Rub together using your finger tips to a breadcrumb consistency. Mix through the whole egg until it starts to form a dough. Turn out onto a floured surface and knead enough to form a smooth dough. Place into the refrigerator for 20 minutes to rest.

3. Remove from the refrigerator and roll out to around 2mm thickness. Place into the tart case and push into the edge of the tin.

4. Prick the base of the tart with a fork and line with grease proof paper weighed down with baking beans. Bake in the oven for 12-15 minutes until crisp and golden, remove the greaseproof paper for the last 5 minutes. Trim the edge and set aside to cool.

5. Whip the cream until thickened but not fully whipped. Fold through the lemon juice before spooning into the cooled tart case.

6. Top the cream with the fresh fruit and garnish with the mint leaves before serving.

Jam Swiss roll

SERVES: 6 | PREP TIME: 30 MINUTES | COOKING TIME: 12 MINUTES

INGREDIENTS

100 g / 3 ½ oz / ⅔ cup self-raising flour

1 tsp baking powder

100 g / 3 ½ oz / ½ cup caster (superfine) sugar

100 g / 3 ½ oz/ ½ cup butter

2 large eggs

225 g / 8 oz / ⅔ cup strawberry jam (jelly)

icing (confectioner's) sugar for dusting

TO SERVE:

2 tbsp strawberry jam (jelly), sieved

150 g / 5 ½ oz / 1 cup strawberries, quartered

1 mango, peeled, stoned and cut into bite-sized chunks

METHOD

1. Preheat the oven to 180°C (160°C fan) / 350F / gas 4 and grease and line a Swiss roll tin with greaseproof paper.

2. Put the flour, baking powder, sugar, butter and eggs in a large mixing bowl and whisk together with an electric whisk for 4 minutes or until pale and well whipped.

3. Spoon the mixture into the tin and spread into an even layer with a palette knife. Bake for 12 minutes or until the cake is springy to the touch.

4. Dust a sheet of greaseproof paper with icing sugar. When the cake is ready, turn it out onto the paper and peel off the lining paper. Spread the cake with the jam, then roll it up tightly and leave to cool.

5. Cut the cake into twelve slices and serve two slices on each plate.

6. Put the jam in a small paper piping bag and pipe a little on each plate, then garnish with strawberries and mango and dust lightly with icing sugar.

Chocolate fondant puddings

SERVES: 4 | PREP TIME: 30 MINUTES | COOKING TIME: 8 MINUTES

INGREDIENTS

90 g / 3 oz / ⅓ cup caster (superfine) sugar

150 g / 5 oz / ⅔ cup butter

150 g / 5 oz / ⅔ cup dark chocolate, chopped

3 egg yolks

3 eggs

1 tbsp plain (all-purpose) flour

1 tsp vanilla extract

METHOD

1. Preheat the oven to 180°C (160°C fan) / 350F / gas 4. Grease four individual dariole moulds.

2. Place the sugar, butter and chocolate in a bowl set over a pan of simmering water and stir occasionally until melted. Remove from the heat and whisk to combine. Leave to cool for 5 minutes.

3. Add the egg yolks and eggs and beat well to combine, then fold in the flour.

4. Pour into the moulds and chill for 20 minutes.

5. Place on a baking tray and cook for 8 minutes.

Lemon sorbet

MAKES: 1 LITRE | PREP TIME: 10 MINUTES

INGREDIENTS

500 g / 1 lb / 2 cups caster
(superfine) sugar

250 ml / 9 fl. oz / 1 cup lemon juice

1 lemon, grated zest

METHOD

1. Heat the sugar in a pan with 750 ml / 1 ⅓
   pints / 3 cups water and stir until dissolved.

2. If the lemon is waxed, dip into boiling water
   briefly to remove it. Stir in the lemon juice
   and zest, then leave to cool.

3. Churn in an ice cream machine to a smooth
   sorbet. Freeze until required.

4. Transfer to the refrigerator 1 hour
   before eating.

Lemon meringue pie

SERVES: 6 | PREP TIME: 1 HOUR | COOKING TIME: 1 HOUR 10 MINUTES

INGREDIENTS

125 g / 4 oz / ½ cup plain (all-purpose) flour

60 g / 2 oz / ¼ cup butter

pinch of salt

cold water

FOR THE FILLING:

3 level tbsp cornflour

60 g / 2 oz / ¼ cup caster (superfine) sugar

300 ml / 10 fl. oz / 1 ¼ cups cold water

grated zest and juice of 2–3 lemons

2 egg yolks

40 g butter

FOR THE MERINGUE:

2 egg whites

120 g / 4 oz / ½ cup caster (superfine) sugar

METHOD

1. Preheat the oven to 190°C (170°C fan) / 370F / gas 5.

2. Make the pastry: sieve the flour and salt into a large bowl, then work the fat into the flour with the pads of your fingers until the mixture resembles breadcrumbs.

3. Work in 2 tablespoons of water and bring the mixture together with a knife, cutting it through to mix, using enough water to just make a smooth ball of dough. Wrap the dough in cling film and refrigerate.

4. Roll the pastry to just larger than your pie dish. Cut an 8 mm strip all round, dampen the rim of the dish and press the pastry strip on to it. Line the tin with the pastry. Prick the base with a fork and bake for 25 minutes.

5. Place the cornflour and sugar in a bowl and add enough of the water to make a smooth paste. Pour the remaining water into a pan with the lemon zest. Bring to the boil, pour onto the cornflour paste and mix.

6. Tip back into the pan and bring back to the boil for 1 minute. Remove from the heat and beat in the egg yolks, lemon juice and butter. Pour into the pastry shell and spread evenly.

7. Whisk the egg whites until stiff, then beat in sugar at a time until thick and glossy. Spread over the filling, sealing the top completely.

8. Reduce the oven heat to 150°C (130°C fan) / 300F / gas 2 and bake for 45 minutes.

Victoria sponge

SERVES: 6-8 | PREP TIME: 40 MINUTES | COOKING TIME: 25 MINUTES

INGREDIENTS

120 g / 4 oz / ½ cup butter,
at room temperature

120 g / 4 oz / ½ cup caster
(superfine) sugar

2 eggs

1 tsp vanilla extract

120 g / 4 oz / ½ cup self-raising flour

raspberry or strawberry jam (jelly)

icing (confectioner's) sugar

METHOD

1. Preheat the oven to 170°C (150°C fan) / 325F / gas 3. Grease and line two 17 cm (7 in) sponge tins.

2. Cream the butter and sugar together until pale and creamy.

3. Whisk the eggs thoroughly, then beat into the butter mixture a little at a time.

4. Stir in the vanilla extract, then sieve the flour a little at a time into the bowl and fold in with a metal spoon. If the batter is a little thick, add a little hot water to loosen.

5. Spoon into the tins, then bake for 25 minutes.

6. Leave to cool for 10 minutes. Remove from the tins and cool on a wire rack. Sandwich with the jam and dust with icing sugar.

Sticky toffee pudding

SERVES: 6 | PREP TIME: 20 MINUTES | COOKING TIME: 40 MINUTES

INGREDIENTS

FOR THE SPONGE:
75 g / 2 ½ oz / ⅓ cup dates, stoned and chopped

1 tsp bicarbonate of soda

50 g / 1 ¾ oz / ¼ cup butter

150 g / 5 oz / ⅔ cup demerara sugar

2 eggs

175 g / 6 oz / ¾ cup self-raising flour

1 tsp vanilla extract

butter, softened

FOR THE SAUCE:
250 ml / 9 fl. oz / 1 cup double
(heavy) cream

80 g / 2 ½ oz / ⅓ cup butter

80 g / 2 ½ oz / ⅓ cup dark brown sugar

METHOD

1. Preheat the oven to 180°C (160°C fan) / 350F / gas 4.

2. Pour 275 ml / 10 fl. oz / 1 cup boiling water into a bowl and add the dates to soak.

3. When the water is lukewarm, add the remaining sponge ingredients, mixing well to combine. Pour into a buttered baking dish and bake in the oven for about 40 minutes, or until just firm.

4. Heat the sauce ingredients in a pan, whisking regularly. When the sponge is cooked, pour over the sauce and flash briefly under a hot grill until bubbling.

5. Serve with ice cream or cream.

White chocolate mousse

SERVES: 4 | PREP TIME: 50 MINUTES

INGREDIENTS

100 g / 3 ½ oz / ½ cup good quality white chocolate, broken into pieces

250 ml / 9 oz / 1 cup double (heavy) cream

2 egg whites

1 tbsp caster (superfine) sugar

2 tbsp white chocolate shavings

METHOD

1. Break the chocolate into small pieces and place in a bowl with the cream. Place over a pan of simmering water and whisk until the chocolate has melted. Remove from the heat, leave to cool and then chill for at least 30 minutes.

2. Whisk the egg whites, adding the sugar as you whisk, until thick and glossy. Whisk the chocolate mixture until the mixture forms soft peaks, then fold the egg whites in a third at a time, being careful not to lose the air.

3. Spoon into ramekins or dessert glasses and chill in the refrigerator until needed.

4. Serve garnished with shavings of white chocolate.

Gingerbread men

MAKES: 10-12 | PREP TIME: 50 MINUTES | COOKING TIME: 12 MINUTES

INGREDIENTS

30 g butter, softened

25 g caster (superfine) sugar

½ tsp bicarbonate of soda

25 g golden syrup

1 egg yolk

125 g / 4 oz / ½ cup plain
(all-purpose) flour

1 tsp ground ginger

½ tsp mixed spice

mixed sugar balls for decoration

golden syrup

METHOD

1. Preheat the oven to 180°C (160°C fan) / 350F /
   gas 4. Whisk together the butter and sugar
   until pale, then stir in the bicarbonate, syrup
   and egg yolk.

2. Sieve in the flour and spices, then mix until
   the mixture comes together in a ball. Roll
   into a cylinder, wrap in cling film and chill
   in the refrigerator for 30 minutes.

3. Roll out to 1 cm (½ in) thickness and cut out
   gingerbread men with appropriate cutters.
   Place them evenly on a lined baking sheet.

4. Bake in the oven for about
   12 minutes, then remove to a wire rack and
   leave to cool. Use the syrup as glue if
   necessary to decorate.

169

Vanilla baked egg custard

MAKES: 4 | PREP TIME: 10 MINUTES | COOKING TIME: 50-60 MINUTES

INGREDIENTS

500 ml / 1 pint / 2 cups milk

1 tsp vanilla extract

40 g caster (superfine) sugar

3 eggs, lightly beaten

grated nutmeg

METHOD

1. Preheat the oven to 180°C (160°C fan) / 350F / gas 5.

2. Heat the milk and vanilla in a pan until nearly at boiling point then set aside to cool for a minute.

3. Meanwhile whisk the sugar with the eggs.

4. Pour the scented milk over the eggs, whisking continually until thickened and smooth.

5. Strain into a buttered oven-proof 1 pint baking dish. Bake for 50–60 minutes until just set.

6. Serve with freshly grated nutmeg over the top.

Banana bread

SERVES: 8 | PREP TIME: 15 MINUTES | COOKING TIME: 50 MINUTES

INGREDIENTS

125 g / 4 ½ oz / 1 ¼ cups rolled porridge oats

125 g / 4 ½ oz / 1 ¼ cups ground almonds

100 g / 3 ½ oz / ½ cup coconut sugar

200 g / 7 oz / 1 ⅓ cups gluten-free plain
(all-purpose) flour

3 tsp baking powder

3 very ripe bananas, mashed

1 egg, beaten

175 ml / 6 fl. oz / ⅔ cup soya milk

50 ml / 1 ¾ fl. oz / ¼ cup coconut oil, melted

sliced bananas to serve

METHOD

1. Preheat the oven to 180°C (160°C fan) / 350F /
   gas 4 and oil and line a large loaf tin with
   greaseproof paper.

2. Put the oats in a food processor and blitz to a
   powder. Add the ground almonds, coconut
   sugar, flour and baking powder and blend
   again briefly to mix.

3. Add the bananas, egg, soya milk and coconut
   oil and pulse until smoothly combined, then
   scrape into the tin.

4. Bake for 50 minutes or until a skewer
   inserted in the centre comes out clean. Leave
   to cool completely on a wire rack before
   slicing and serving with sliced banana.

Crème brûlée

SERVES: 4 | PREP TIME: 2 HOURS | COOKING TIME: 30 MINUTES

INGREDIENTS

450 ml / 1 pint / 2 cups double (heavy) cream

100 ml / 3 ½ fl. oz / ½ cup milk

1 vanilla pod, halved

5 egg yolks

2 tbsp caster (superfine) sugar plus enough for the topping

1 strawberry, thinly sliced

1 handful blueberries, washed

1 sprig of mint

METHOD

1. Preheat the oven to 180°C (160°C fan) / 350F / gas 5.

2. Tip the cream into a pan with the milk. Add the seeds from the vanilla pod and the pod itself. Heat almost to boiling point.

3. Whisk the egg yolks and sugar in a bowl until pale in colour. Pour the hot cream into the egg yolks, whisking constantly. Strain through a sieve and stir well.

4. Sit four ramekins in a roasting tin and divide the mixture evenly between them. Pour in enough hot water to come half way up the sides of the ramekins.

5. Bake for about 30 minutes, until set.

6. Leave to cool on a wire rack, then refrigerate until ready to serve.

7. Sprinkle over a thick layer of sugar and either grill or blowtorch until deep golden and melted. Leave until cool and firm, then serve garnished with the sliced strawberry, blueberries and mint.

Crème caramel

SERVES: 4 | PREP TIME: 25 MINUTES | COOKING TIME: 1 HOUR

INGREDIENTS

125 g / 4 oz / ½ cup caster
(superfine) sugar

2 tbsp hot water

150 ml / 5 fl. oz / ⅔ cup milk

300 ml / 10 fl. oz / 1 cup single cream

4 eggs

40 g soft dark brown sugar

2 drops vanilla extract

METHOD

1. Preheat the oven to 150°C (130°C fan) / 300F / gas 2.

2. Place the sugar in a stainless steel pan and heat. When the sugar begins to melt, leave to darken to a rich dark gold. Do not stir. Remove from the heat, carefully add the water, and pour into a soufflé dish.

3. Pour the milk and cream into a pan and heat gently.

4. Whisk the eggs, sugar and vanilla in a bowl. When the milk is very hot but not boiling, pour onto the egg mixture, whisking constantly until completely blended.

5. Pour into the soufflé dish and place in a roasting tin. Pour in enough hot water to come two thirds of the way up the sides of the dish.

6. Bake in the oven for 1 hour until set.

7. Remove from the refrigerator 1 hour before serving, then release carefully form the mould onto a plate.

Vanilla custard

SERVES: 4 | PREP TIME: 5 MINUTES | COOKING TIME: 10 MINUTES

INGREDIENTS

300 ml / 10 fl. oz / 1 ¼ cups single cream

3 egg yolks

1 tsp cornflour

1 tbsp caster (superfine) sugar

½ tsp vanilla extract

METHOD

1. Heat the cream in a pan until nearly boiling.

2. Whisk the egg yolks, cornflour, sugar and vanilla extract.

3. Pour the hot cream into the bowl, whisking all the time, then return to the pan. Whisk over a low heat until the sauce has thickened.

4. If the sauce does start to curdle, simply remove from the heat and whisk vigorously as it cools. It will become smooth again.

5. Delicious served with pies and crumbles.

Millionaire's shortbread

MAKES: 4 | SERVES: 4 | PREP TIME: 25 MINUTES | COOKING TIME: 25-35 MINUTES

INGREDIENTS

225 g / 8 oz / 1 ½ cups plain (all-purpose) flour

75 g / 2 ½ oz / ⅓ cup caster (superfine) sugar

150 g / 5 oz / ⅔ cup butter, cubed

FOR THE TOPPING:

400 g / 14 oz / 1 ⅔ cups can of condensed milk

200 g / 7 oz / 1 ⅓ cups milk chocolate, chopped

50 g / 1 ¾ oz / ½ cup butter

METHOD

1. Make the caramel layer in advance. Put the unopened can of condensed milk in a saucepan of water and simmer for 3 hours, adding more water as necessary to ensure it doesn't boil dry. Leave the can to cool completely, then chill in the fridge.

2. Preheat the oven to 180°C (160°C fan) / 350F / gas 4 and line a 20 cm (8 in) square cake tin with greaseproof paper.

Lemon drizzle cake

SERVES: 6 | PREP TIME: 25 MINUTES | COOKING TIME: 40-45 MINUTES

INGREDIENTS

120 g / 4 oz / ½ cup butter, softened

175 g / 6 oz / ¾ cup caster
(superfine) sugar

2 eggs

1 lemon, grated zest

175 g / 6 oz / ¾ cup self-raising flour

100 ml / 3 ½ fl. oz / ½ cup milk

FOR THE SYRUP:

2 lemons, juiced

100 g / 3 ½ oz / ½ cup icing (confectioner's) sugar

FOR THE GLAZE:

½ lemon, juiced

150 g / 5 oz / ⅔ cup icing
(confectioner's) sugar

METHOD

1. Preheat the oven to 180°C (160°C fan) / 350F / gas 4. Grease and line a loaf tin.

2. Cream the butter and sugar until pale and creamy, then whisk in the eggs a little at a time.

3. Whisk in the zest, then, using a metal spoon, fold in the flour, salt and then stir in the milk. Spoon into the loaf tin and bake for 40–45 minutes until a skewer comes out clean when poked into the centre. Set aside.

4. Heat the lemon juice and sugar in a pan until the sugar dissolves.

5. Puncture the surface of the cake with a skewer and pour over the hot syrup. Leave to cool completely then remove from the tin.

6. Whisk together the lemon juice and sugar to make the glaze, then drizzle over the top of the cake.

Chocolate chip cookies

MAKES: 12-16 | PREP TIME: 20 MINUTES | COOKING TIME: 20-25 MINUTES

INGREDIENTS

120 g / 4 oz / ½ cup dark chocolate, chopped

150 g / 5 oz / ⅔ cup plain
(all-purpose) flour

1 tbsp cocoa powder

1 tsp bicarbonate of (baking) soda

pinch of salt

120 g / 4 oz / ½ cup butter, softened

120 g / 4 oz / ½ cup caster
(superfine) sugar

1 egg

350 g / 12 oz / 1 ½ cups chocolate chips, white or dark

METHOD

1. Preheat the oven to 170°C (150°C fan) / 325F / gas 3.

2. Place the chocolate in a bowl over a pan over simmering water and stir until melted. Set aside to cool.

3. Tip the flour, cocoa powder and bicarbonate into a bowl and stir in the salt.

4. Cream the butter and sugar in a bowl until pale and creamy, then whisk in the melted chocolate.

5. Whisk in the egg, then the dry ingredients, then the chocolate chips.

6. Splodge fairly even amounts onto a lined baking sheet about 6 cm (3 ½ in) apart. Cook for 20 minutes or until an inserted skewer comes out not wet with batter – it won't be clean.

7. Leave to cool then transfer to a wire rack. Best eaten warm and soft.

Cherry clafoutis

SERVES: 6-8 | PREP TIME: 5 MINUTES | COOKING TIME: 35-40 MINUTES

INGREDIENTS

500 g / 1 lb / 2 cups cherries, stoned

125 g / 4 oz / ½ cup plain
(all-purpose) flour

pinch of salt

50 g / 1 ¾ oz / ¼ cup caster
(superfine) sugar

3 eggs, beaten

300 ml / 10 fl. oz / 1 ¼ cups milk

METHOD

1. Preheat the oven to 180°C (160°C fan) / 350F / gas 5.

2. Grease a baking tin with butter or vegetable oil, then place the cherries in the bottom.

3. In a bowl, whisk together the flour, salt and sugar and the beaten eggs until smooth, then whisk in the milk and mix to a smooth batter.

4. Pour the mixture over the cherries and bake for 35–40 minutes.

5. Allow to cool before serving.

Black Forest gateau

SERVES: 4 | PREP TIME: I HOUR | COOKING TIME: 25 MINUTES

INGREDIENTS

250 g / 9 oz / 1 cup butter, softened

250 g / 9 oz / 1 cup caster (superfine) sugar

150 g / 5 oz / ⅔ cup self-raising flour

3 tbsp cocoa powder

I tsp baking powder

4 eggs

350 g / 12 oz / 1 ½ cups morello cherry jam (jelly)

1 jar or can bottled cherries and their juice

3 tbsp Kirsch

500 ml / 1 pint / 2 cups double (heavy) cream

50 g / 1 ¾ oz / ¼ cup dark chocolate, grated

METHOD

1. Preheat the oven to 190°C (170°C fan) / 375F / gas 5. Grease and line two 20 x 20 cm (8 in) sandwich tins.

2. Mix the butter, sugar, flour, cocoa powder, baking powder and eggs in a food processor until smooth.

3. Divide equally between the bake tins and bake for 25 minutes until risen. Turn onto a wire rack. Leave to cool completely. Slice the cakes in half horizontally.

4. Heat the jam with the cherries and Kirsch for 5 minutes. Leave to cool. Spread over three of the sponges. Whisk 300 ml / 10 fl. oz of the cream to soft peaks.

5. Transfer a cherry-topped sponge to a plate, then smooth on ⅓ of the cream. Sprinkle with chocolate.

6. Top with a cherry-topped sponge and repeat, then with the third sponge. Place the final clean sponge on top.

7. Whisk the cream to soft peaks. Smooth over the cake top and sides with a palette knife. Finish with grated chocolate.

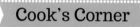
Cook's Bible

Sides, snacks and more

Pepper salad

SERVES: 2 | PREP TIME: 15 MINUTES

INGREDIENTS

1 red pepper

1 yellow pepper

½ cucumber

100 g / 3 ½ oz. mixed crisp salad leaves

1 lemon, juiced

50 ml / 1 ¾ fl. oz / ¼ cup extra virgin olive oil

1 tsp Dijon mustard

1 garlic clove, minced

Salt and freshly ground black pepper

METHOD

1. Cut the peppers in half and remove the seeds before slicing.

2. Peel strips from the skin of the cucumber and discard. Slice the cucumber.

3. Combine the peppers, cucumber and salad leaves in a mixing bowl.

4. Combine the lemon, oil, mustard and garlic in a small jar with a lid. Shake well to combine and season with salt and black pepper to taste.

5. Pour the dressing over the salad and toss.

6. Place the salad into serving bowls.

188

Taramasalata

SERVES: 6-8 | PREP TIME: 10 MINUTES

INGREDIENTS

250 g / 9 oz. smoked fish roe

75 g / 2 ½ oz. stale bread

25 g / 1 oz. / ¼ cup almonds

1 lemon, juiced

200 ml / 7 fl. oz / ¾ cup extra virgin olive oil

Salt and cracked black pepper

A handful of flat leaf parsley, chopped

Toasted pitta breads to serve

METHOD

1. Place the fish roe, bread, almonds, lemon juice and a splash of water into a blender. Pulse gently to chop and combine the ingredients.

2. Gradually add the oil blending after each addition until you have the desired consistency. It should be fairly thick but smooth. Season to taste with salt and freshly ground black pepper.

3. Serve in a bowl with the parsley sprinkled over the top and a drop more oil drizzled on the surface. Great as a pre-dinner snack when served with toasted pitta breads or as part of a mezze platter.

Greek salad

SERVES: 4 | PREP TIME: 40 MINUTES

INGREDIENTS

150 g / 5 oz / ⅔ cup cherry tomatoes

1 cucumber

1 red onion, halved and finely sliced

150 g / 5 oz / ⅔ cup black olives, stoned

200 g / 7 oz / ¾ cup feta cheese

2–3 tbsp red wine vinegar

1 tsp dried oregano or small handful fresh oregano leaves

6–8 tbsp extra virgin olive oil

METHOD

1. Halve the cherry tomatoes and place in a bowl with a little salt and a drizzle of olive oil. Leave for up to 30 minutes.

2. Halve the cucumber lengthways, then scrape out the seeds with a teaspoon. Slice the halves into half-moons, then place in a colander, sprinkle with a little salt and leave to drain for 30 minutes. Combine in a large salad bowl with the olives and crumble in the feta cheese.

3. In a separate bowl, whisk together the vinegar and a little seasoning and the oregano and some extra virgin olive oil.

4. Drizzle the dressing over the salad vegetables and toss thoroughly before serving.

Pilau rice

SERVES: 4 | PREP TIME: 30 MINUTES | COOKING TIME: 15 MINUTES

INGREDIENTS

500 g / 1 lb / 2 cups basmati rice

30 g butter

1 onion, peeled and finely chopped

5 cardamom pods, lightly crushed

1 cinnamon stick

6 cloves

saffron soaked in 500 ml / 1 pint / 2 cups
vegetable stock

a pinch of salt

METHOD

1. Wash the rice in a sieve under cold running
   water, then leave to soak for 30 minutes.

2. Heat the butter in a pan and when foaming
   add the onion. Cook until golden and sweet.

3. Add the spices and toast lightly, then tip in the
   rice and stir well to coat in the butter.

4. Pour over the stock and a little salt, bring to
   the boil and cover with a lid. Turn the heat
   down and leave to cook for 9–10 minutes.

5. Turn off the heat and leave to stand for 5
   minutes. Remove the lid and stir with
   a fork to separate the grains.

6. Great served with curry.

191

Scotch eggs

SERVES: 4 | PREP TIME: 30 MINUTES | COOKING TIME: 10 MINUTES

INGREDIENTS

4 good quality pork sausages, skins removed

4 eggs, cooked and shells removed,
plus 1 raw egg

4 tbsp plain (all-purpose) flour

75 g / 2 ½ oz / ½ cup panko breadcrumbs

3 litres / 5 pints / 12 cups sunflower oil

METHOD

1. Divide the sausage meat into 4 balls. Flatten one ball of sausage meat onto your hand and put an egg in the centre, then squeeze the meat round the outside to coat. Repeat this process with the other 3 cooked eggs.

2. Put the flour, raw egg and panko breadcrumbs in three separate bowls.

3. Dip the scotch eggs in the flour, then in the egg, then in the breadcrumbs.

4. Heat the oil in a deep fat fryer, according to the manufacturer's instructions, to a temperature of 180°C. Lower the scotch eggs in the fryer basket and cook for 4-5 minutes or until crisp and golden brown.

Breaded mushrooms

SERVES: 4 | PREP TIME: 15 MINUTES | COOKING TIME: 20 MINUTES

INGREDIENTS

100 g / 3 ½ oz / ½ cup button mushrooms, cleaned

100 g / 3 ½ oz / ½ cup plain
(all-purpose) flour, seasoned

1 tsp mustard powder

2 eggs, beaten

100 g / 3 ½ oz / ½ cup fine breadcrumbs

2 tbsp Parmesan, finely grated

vegetable oil for deep frying

METHOD

1. Lay the flour, eggs and breadcrumbs out in separate dishes, adding the mustard powder to the flour and Parmesan to the breadcrumbs.

2. Dip the mushrooms one by one into each dish, coating thoroughly.

3. Heat the oil to 180°C / 350F and deep fry the mushrooms a few at a time until golden brown all over.

4. Drain on kitchen paper and serve.

193

Ultimate mashed potato

SERVES: 4 | PREP TIME: 2 MINUTES | COOKING TIME: 40 MINUTES

INGREDIENTS

1 kg / 2 ¼ lb / 4 ¼ cups floury potatoes such as King Edward or Desiree

100 g / 3 ½ oz / ½ cup butter

75–100 ml / 2 ½–3 ½ oz / ⅓ – ½ cup milk, warmed

salt and pepper

METHOD

1. Cook the potatoes whole in their skins in boiling salted water until tender all the way through – about 30 minutes, but keep checking.

2. Drain thoroughly and leave to cool for 5 minutes, then peel off the skins while still hot.

3. Return the flesh to the pan, mash finely and stir in the butter and enough milk with a wooden spoon to make a light, creamy, smooth mash.

4. Season generously and serve hot.

194

Potato salad

SERVES: 4 | PREP TIME: 5 MINUTES | COOKING TIME: 20 MINUTES

INGREDIENTS

1 kg / 2 ¼ lb / 4 ¼ cups new or salad potatoes
(such as Anya or Charlotte)

2 sprigs mint

a pinch of salt

200 g / 7 oz / ¾ cup mayonnaise

½ bunch chives, chopped

2 spring onions (scallions), chopped

½ bunch parsley, chopped

salt and pepper

METHOD

1. Cook the potatoes whole in boiling salted water with the mint sprigs, covered with a lid, for about 20 minutes or until tender.

2. Drain thoroughly.

3. Leave to cool slightly then slice thickly.

4. Mix the mayonnaise with the herbs and seasoning and toss with the potatoes while still warm.

Arancini with tomato and mozzarella

SERVES: 4 | PREP TIME: 20 MINUTES | COOKING TIME: 10 MINUTES

INGREDIENTS

60 g / 2 oz / ¼ cup leftover risotto rice, cooked

1 tbsp Parmesan, grated

1 tomato, seeded and finely diced

1 ball mozzarella, cut into small cubes

½ bunch basil leaves

1 tbsp plain (all-purpose) flour

1 egg, beaten

40 g breadcrumbs

vegetable oil, for deep frying

METHOD

1. Leave the leftover risotto to get completely cold – preferably refrigerated overnight.

2. Stir the tomato and Parmesan through the risotto. Shape into equal balls, pushing a small cube of mozzarella into the centre of each and shaping the rice around it.

3. Lay out the flour, egg and breadcrumbs on separate plates. Dip the balls into the flour, then the egg, then the breadcrumbs. Use one hand and keep the other clean for ease.

4. Heat the oil to 180°C or until a cube of bread sizzles when dunked in.

5. Fry the risotto balls until golden and crisp all over. Drain on kitchen paper.

Sautéed new potatoes

SERVES: 4 | PREP TIME: 10 MINUTES | COOKING TIME: 10-15 MINUTES

INGREDIENTS

750 g / 1 ⅓ lb / 3 cups new or salad potatoes such as
Charlotte or Anya

5 tbsp olive oil

salt and pepper

½ bunch thyme leaves

2 cloves garlic

METHOD

1. Parboil the potatoes in salted water for 6 minutes or so, until they begin to soften.

2. Drain thoroughly, set back over a low heat to drive off any excess moisture.

3. Use the end of a rolling pin to lightly crack or crush the potatoes to create crisp edges in the pan.

4. Heat the oil in a pan large enough to hold them in one layer, then add the potatoes.

5. Season well, toss in the thyme and garlic and sauté for around 10–15 minutes until golden and crisp.

Coleslaw

SERVES: 4-6 | PREP TIME: 40 MINUTES

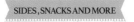

INGREDIENTS

¼ white cabbage, finely shredded

¼ red cabbage, finely shredded

a pinch of salt

½ red onion, finely sliced

2 carrots, peeled and grated

1 apple, peeled and cut into
fine matchsticks

FOR THE DRESSING:

6 tbsp mayonnaise

2 tbsp sour cream

2 tbsp grain mustard

1 tbsp lemon juice

METHOD

1. Salt the shredded cabbage in a bowl and set
aside for 30 minutes.

2. Drain off any excess liquid, then tip into a
large bowl.

3. Add the onion, carrots and apple.

4. Mix together the ingredients for the
dressing with seasoning and toss the salad
thoroughly in it.

5. Serve within 2 hours.

Hummus

SERVES: 4-6 | PREP TIME: 10 MINUTES

INGREDIENTS

400 g / 14 oz canned chickpeas (garbanzo beans)

2 cloves of garlic

1 tbsp tahini

1 tsp ground coriander (cilantro)

1 tsp ground cumin

100 ml / 3 ½ fl. oz / ½ cup olive oil

1 lemon, juice and zest

Sea salt and cracked black pepper

1 tsp paprika

Pita breads to serve

METHOD

1. Drain the chickpeas and add to the cup of a blender.

2. Add the garlic, tahini, coriander, cumin and half the olive oil. Blend for a minute until smooth, stopping occasionally to scrape the ingredients from the edge of the blender. Add a more of the oil gradually until you have the desired consistency, you may not need it all.

3. Season with salt and black pepper to taste and stir through the lemon juice.

4. Spoon into a serving bowl and top with paprika and an additional drizzle of oil. Serve with toasted pitta breads to dip.

Homemade chips

SERVES: 4 | PREP TIME: 10 MINUTES | COOKING TIME: 10-15 MINUTES

INGREDIENTS

4 large baking potatoes, peeled and cut into
1 cm (½ in) thick batons

vegetable oil

salt

METHOD

1. To make the chips, soak well in cold water to remove the starch then dry thoroughly.

2. Bring a pan a third full of oil to 140°C / 275F and plunge in the chips, in batches if necessary and cook for 10 minutes until pale but starting to look 'cooked'.

3. Remove, drain on kitchen paper.

4. Heat the oil to 180°C / 350F and plunge the chips back in until golden and crisp. Remove to kitchen paper, season well and serve hot.

Mushy peas

SERVES: 4 | PREP TIME: 5 MINUTES | COOKING TIME: 10 MINUTES

INGREDIENTS

4 tbsp olive oil

500 g / 1 lb / 2 cups frozen peas

3 spring onions, (scallions), finely chopped

1 bunch mint leaves, chopped

salt and pepper

1 tsp sugar

30 g butter

METHOD

1. Heat the olive oil gently in a pan and add the peas and spring onions.

2. Cook until they turn bright vivid green, then add the mint, seasoning and a little sugar.

3. Crush with a potato masher and add the butter, and serve hot.

Guacamole

SERVES: 5 | PREP TIME: 5 MINUTES

INGREDIENTS

3 ripe avocados, peeled and stoned

1 small onion, grated

1 Jalapeno, deseeded and finely chopped

2 tomatoes, deseeded and diced

1 lime, juiced

tortilla chips, to serve

METHOD

1. Mash the avocados with a fork until fairly smooth.

2. Stir in the onion, Jalapeno, tomato and lime juice and season to taste with plenty of salt and pepper.

3. Scrape the mixture into a serving bowl and serve with tortilla chips for dipping.

Classic hollandaise sauce

SERVES: 4 | PREP TIME: 5 MINUTES | COOKING TIME: 10-15 MINUTES

INGREDIENTS

2 tbsp white wine vinegar

2 tbsp water

1 slice onion

pinch ground mace

1 bay leaf

6 black peppercorns, left whole

3 egg yolks

180 g / 6 oz / ¾ cup butter at room temperature

squeeze of lemon juice

salt and white pepper

METHOD

1. Place the vinegar, water, onion, mace, bay leaf and peppercorns in a small pan and reduce to about 1 tbsp. Strain into a bowl, add 1 tablespoon of water.

2. Whisk the egg yolks into the reduction.

3. Place the bowl over a pan of barely simmering water and add a little of the butter, whisking until it has melted.

4. Add the butter a little at a time, whisking continually, until the mixture emulsifies and thickens.

5. Cook very gently for 2 minutes, then add a little lemon juice and season.

Oven-baked wedges

SERVES: 4 | PREP TIME: 15 MINUTES | COOKING TIME: 30 MINUTES

INGREDIENTS

4 large floury potatoes, scrubbed

5 tbsp olive oil

salt

1 tsp paprika

pinch of cayenne pepper

½ tsp celery salt

1 tsp dried oregano

tomato relish or chutney, to serve

METHOD

1. Preheat the oven to 220°C (200°C fan) / 450F / gas 7.

2. Cut the potatoes into wedges lengthways. Parboil in salted water for 3–4 minutes.

3. Drain thoroughly, then set back over a low heat to drive off any excess moisture.

4. Place on a baking sheet and toss with the oil and seasonings until thoroughly coated.

5. Bake in the oven for about 30 minutes until deep gold and crisp.

6. Drain briefly on kitchen paper.

205

Cranberry sauce

SERVES: 4 | PREP TIME: 5 MINUTES | COOKING TIME: 10-15 MINUTES

INGREDIENTS

500 g / 1 lb / 2 cups fresh cranberries

200 g / 7 oz / ¾ cup sugar

zest and juice of 1 orange

1 tbsp port or cassis

METHOD

1. Place the ingredients in a pan and add 4 tablespoons of water.

2. Bring to a boil then reduce the heat and cook until the cranberries have burst and the sauce has thickened.

3. Pour into a bowl and check if it needs more sugar – it will thicken further as it cools.

Pesto

MAKES: 100ML | PREP TIME: 10 MINUTES

INGREDIENTS

2 handfuls pine nuts

1 clove garlic, peeled and chopped

2 bunches basil

80 g / 3 oz / ⅓ cup Parmesan, grated

extra virgin olive oil

salt and pepper

METHOD

1. Add the pine nuts to a frying pan over medium heat and lightly toast for a few seconds until golden.

2. Place in a food processor with the garlic, basil and Parmesan.

3. Whizz the ingredients in a food processor until roughly blended, stirring in enough olive oil to loosen.

4. This pesto will keep in the refrigerator for up to three days.

Rustic potato wedges

SERVES: 2-4 | PREP TIME: 10 MINUTES | COOKING TIME: 40 MINUTES

INGREDIENTS

500 g / 1 lb 1 oz Maris Piper potatoes, peeled and quartered

100 g / 3 ½ oz goose fat or lard

salt and cracked black pepper

1 tsp dried oregano

1 tsp dried rosemary

1 red onion, quartered

METHOD

1. Preheat the oven to 220°C (200°C fan) / 425F / gas 7. Place the fat into a deep sided baking tray and place into the oven to heat up.

2. Place the potatoes into a pan of salted boiling water and cook for 8-10 minutes until tender but still firm. Drain and place onto a wire rack to cool and the moisture to evaporate.

3. Once the potatoes are cool, toss them in the salt, pepper and herbs to coat.

4. Carefully remove the hot pan of fat from the oven and gently place the potato wedges into the hot fat, they should sizzle immediately. Using a spoon turn the oven in the fat so that all sides have been coated.

5. Return to the oven and bake for around 30 minutes until golden and crisp.

6. Remove from the oven and place the potatoes onto kitchen paper using a slotted spoon. Place into a serving dish and garnish with the red onion.

Rustic pesto

SERVES: 4 | PREP TIME: 10 MINUTES

INGREDIENTS

3 large bunches of basil, leaves only

2 cloves of garlic, minced

100 ml / 3 ½ fl. oz / ½ cup extra virgin olive oil

25 g / 1 oz. / ¼ cup pine nuts, toasted

50 g / 1 ¾ oz. / ½ cup parmesan cheese, grated

50 g / 1 ¾ oz. / ½ cup pecorino cheese, grated

1 lemon, juice and zest

1 tbsp sea salt flakes

Cracked black pepper

METHOD

1. Place the basil, garlic, oil, nuts and cheese into a blender and blend until smooth, add more oil if a little thick.

2. Taste and add enough lemon juice, salt and pepper to taste, quickly pulse to combine and taste again.

3. If using immediately then spoon over warm pasta in a hot pan.

4. Alternatively, the pesto will keep in the fridge for a couple of days if a layer of oil is poured over the surface.

Chicken stock

SERVES: 500ML | PREP TIME: 5 MINUTES | COOKING TIME: 3 HOURS

INGREDIENTS

1 chicken carcass, (cooked for better flavour) broken up

1 stick celery

1 carrot, chopped

1 onion, peeled and halved and stuck with 2 cloves

6 black peppercorns

1 bouquet garni

1 leek, white part only, chopped

METHOD

1. Place the bones in a large pan, add the vegetables and cover with water.

2. Bring to the boil, then reduce the heat and leave to cook uncovered for about 3 hours.

3. Skim any fat or scum from the surface from time to time.

4. When done, strain into a large bowl and chill. This will make any fat easy to remove.

5. Store in the refrigerator until needed or freeze for up to three months.

Mint sauce

SERVES: 4 | PREP TIME: 5 MINUTES

INGREDIENTS

1 bunch mint leaves

1 tbsp cider or white wine vinegar

1 clove of garlic, minced

1 tbsp olive oil

½ tsp sugar

½ tsp English mustard

salt and pepper

3–4 tbsp natural yogurt (optional)

METHOD

1. Chop the mint leaves finely and place in a food processor with the vinegar, garlic, oil, sugar and mustard.

2. Whizz to make a thick sauce.

3. Season to taste.

4. Great served with roast lamb. Add the yogurt if you want a creamier sauce.

Apple sauce

SERVES: 4 | PREP TIME: 5 MINUTES | COOKING TIME: 10-15 MINUTES

INGREDIENTS

250 g / 9 oz / 1 cup Bramley apples

250 g / 9 oz / 1 cup Cox apples

1 tbsp sugar (optional, depending on tartness
of apples and usage)

2 cloves

2 tbsp water

METHOD

1. Peel and core the apples and cut into chunks.

2. Place in a pan with the sugar, cloves and
water and cover with a lid.

3. Cook over a low heat for 10–15 minutes,
checking occasionally, until the apples have
'exploded' to a fine purée and are soft.

4. Beat to a purée, remove the cloves and serve.

Vegetable stock

MAKES: 1 PINT | PREP TIME: 5 MINUTES | COOKING TIME: 30 MINUTES

INGREDIENTS

2 sticks celery, chopped

1 onion, peeled and chopped

2 carrots, chopped

2 bay leaves

10 black peppercorns

1 bunch parsley stalks, tied

salt

METHOD

1. Place the vegetables in a pan and cover with 570–850 ml (1–1 ½ pints) cold water.

2. Bring to the boil, reduce the heat and simmer for 30 minutes.

3. Strain. The stock is ready to use.

217

Egg and prawn bites

SERVES: 12 | PREP TIME: 15 MINUTES | COOKING TIME: 10 MINUTES

INGREDIENTS

6 large free range eggs

50 g / 1 ½ oz mayonnaise, gluten free

½ tsp ketchup, gluten free

a pinch of paprika

½ lemon, juiced

50 g / 1 ½ oz prawns (shrimp), cooked

a handful parsley, finely chopped

METHOD

1. Place the eggs into a saucepan and cover with cold water. Bring to the boil over a medium high heat, cover with a lid and turn off the heat. Leave for 8 to 10 minutes, drain and refill with cold water to cool the eggs.

2. While the eggs are cooking, combine the mayonnaise with the ketchup, paprika and lemon juice. Combine and season.

3. Once the eggs have cooled, carefully peel then and cut in half. Gently remove the cooked yolk using a tea spoon and add to the mayonnaise mixture.

4. Spoon the mayonnaise and yolk mixture back into the egg halves and top with a few prawns. Garnish with the chopped parsley.

Tartare sauce

MAKES: 200ML | PREP TIME: 10 MINUTES

INGREDIENTS

200 g / 7 oz / ¾ cup mayonnaise

1 shallot

2 gherkins (cornichons)

2 tbsp capers, drained

½ bunch parsley, chopped

½ lemon, juiced

salt and pepper

METHOD

1. Finely chop the shallot and gherkins.

2. Place all of the ingredients into a bowl, adding the mayonnaise last.

3. Mix well to combine all of the ingredients.

4. Adjust the seasoning to taste using salt and pepper and serve.

219

Fish stock

MAKES: 500ML | PREP TIME: 10 MINUTES | COOKING TIME: 20 MINUTES

INGREDIENTS

450 g / 1 lb / 2 cups fish trimmings
and bones

500 ml / 1 pint / 2 cups water

150 ml / 5 fl. oz / ⅔ cup dry white wine

1 onion, cut into quarters

2 sticks celery, chopped

parsley sprigs

1 bay leaf

salt and pepper

METHOD

1. Place everything in a large pan and bring to
   a simmer.

2. Simmer gently for 20 minutes.

3. Strain and reserve the stock.

Four cheese sauce

SERVES: 4 | PREP TIME: 10 MINUTES | COOKING TIME: 15 MINUTES

INGREDIENTS

1 tbsp butter

½ shallot, finely chopped

1 glass dry white wine

400 ml / 13 ½ fl. oz / 1 ½ cups double (heavy) cream

100 g / 3 ½ oz / ½ cup Gruyère, grated

100 g / 3 ½ oz / ½ cup Parmesan, grated

50 g / 1 ¾ oz / ¼ cup blue cheese,
such as Roquefort crumbled

50 g / 1 ¾ oz / ¼ cup Cheddar, grated

½ tsp mustard powder

METHOD

1. Heat the butter in a pan and sweat the shallot until translucent.

2. Add the white wine and reduce until nearly evaporated.

3. Pour in the cream, heat and stir in the cheeses to melt.

4. Add the mustard powder and season carefully.

221

INDEX